AF609245

A Place for the Birds

The Legacy of Creamer's Field Migratory Waterfowl Refuge

Jessica A. Shepherd, M.A.
Mark D. Ross, Artist

Sandhill Crane Colt

Copyright © 2025 Jessica A.Shepherd.
All rights reserved. Reproduction or translation of any part of this work beyond that permitted by Section 107 or 108 of the 1976 United States Copyright Act without permission in writing from the copyright owner is unlawful.

ISBN 978-1954896727 Hardbound
ISBN 978-1954896734 Paperback
ISBN 978-1954896741 ebook

Library of Congress Control Number: 2025923083

Art by Mark D. Ross
Cover images by Ken Whitten

Publisher's Cataloging-in-Publication Data
Names: Shepherd, Jessica A., author. | Ross, Mark D., artist.
Title: A place for the birds : the legacy of Creamer's Field Migratory Waterfowl Refuge / Jessica A. Shepherd, M.A.; illustrations Mark D. Ross.
Description: Includes bibliographical references and index. | Anchorage, AK: Fathom Publishing Company, 2026.
Identifiers: LCCN: 2025923083 | ISBN: 978-1954896727 (hardcover) | 978-1954896734 (paperback) | 978-1954896741 (ebook)
Subjects: LCSH Birds--Alaska--Creamer's Field Migratory Waterfowl Refuge. | Wildlife refuges--Alaska. | Wildlife refuges--Alaska--History. | Nature conservation--Alaska--History. | Wildlife conservation--Alaska--History. | Wildlife management--Alaska--History. | Dairy farmers--Alaska--Fairbanks--Biography. | Farm life--Alaska--Fairbanks. | BISAC NATURE / Regional | NATURE / Animals / Birds |NATURE / Environmental Conservation & Protection | HISTORY / United States / State & Local / West (AK, CA, CO, HI, ID, MT, NV, UT, WY)
Classification: LCC QH76.5.A4 S44 2025 | DDC 333.951609798--dc23

Fathom Publishing
Anchorage, Alaska
fathompublishing.com

We recognize the Dene People
as the traditional custodians of the Tanana Valley,
and we greatly respect the depth
of their ecological knowledge and
spiritual connection to this sacred place.

Dancing Sandhill Cranes

To all the children of Creamer's Field,
past, present, and future,
may there always be wooded trails,
fleeting birds, and still ponds.

Children explore pond life at Creamer's Field. Friends of Creamer's Field Photo Archives.

Table of Contents

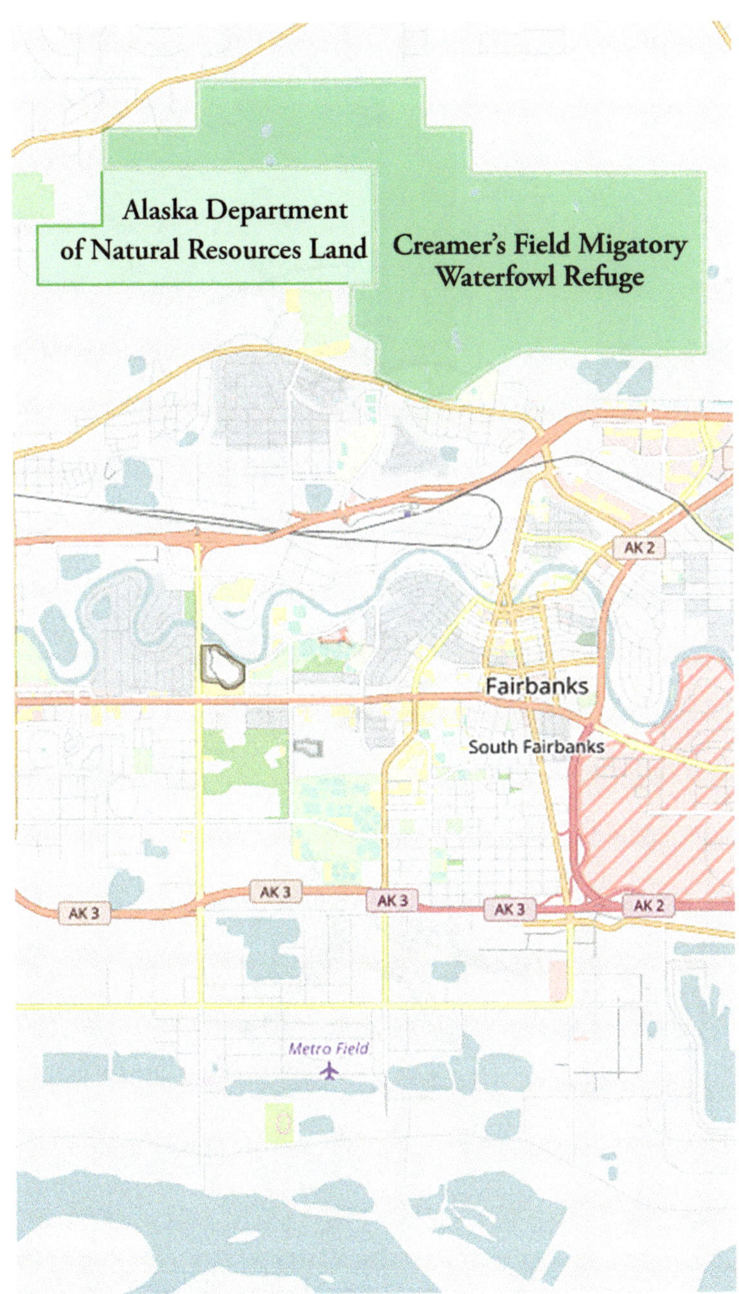

Fairbanks, Alaska and Creamer's Field Migratory Waterfowl Refuge. From OpenStreetMap. https://commons.wikimedia.org/wiki/File:Fairbanks,_Alaska.png.

Sandhill Cranes in Flight

Author's Note

This story details the farming history and ongoing importance of the Creamer's Field Migratory Waterfowl Refuge in Fairbanks, Alaska. More significantly, it highlights the grassroots effort by the community of Fairbanks, working with a kindly old farmer, to preserve open land in the heart of a rapidly expanding city for the benefit of the thousands of migrating cranes, geese, and ducks that rely upon these open fields from early spring until late fall each year. Because of this shared vision, Creamer's Field has become a center for environmental education, outdoor recreation, and biological research while actively providing for the needs of wildlife.

Violet-Green Swallow

Acknowledgements

When I wrote the first edition of *A Place for the Birds* for a master's thesis, completed in December 2003, a number of people provided information, reviewed sections for factual accuracy, and offered encouragement. I would like to especially thank Terrence Cole, Carolyn Kremers, Mary Mangusso, Claus Naske, John Wright, Susan Grace Stoltz, Herb Melchior, Ruth Knapman, Mark D. Ross, Gail Mayo, Donna Krier, Jim Herriges, Mette Moeller, Peggy Hetman, Don and Tracie Pendergrast, Frank Nelson, and, above all, Jeannie Creamer-Dalton for their time and assistance, which they gave so generously.

But the story of the Creamer's dairy and its metamorphosis from farm fields to wildlife refuge doesn't end, and so the book has morphed as well into the volume you now hold in your hands. This edition was only possible because of the determination of Mary Zalar, who blew the dust off the cover of the 2003 volume and found my contact information, and Connie Taylor of Fathom Publishing, who willingly took up the project and made editing it together a joy. We revisited the book, with Mary doing the legwork of contacting ADF&G folks, including Clint Cooper, Nate Lashomb, and retired staff John Wright and Pam Bruce, along with Friends of Creamer's Field staff Grace Nelson, Melanie Graeff, and Lauren Puleo, and Tricia Blake with the Alaska Songbird Institute, who provided updated information on management practices and operations, photos, and the like. Meanwhile, Connie patiently made countless edits, offered suggestions, and crafted the final product into a little gem. It just goes to show that the Creamer's Field Migratory Waterfowl Refuge continues to bring people together out of a common gratitude for wild birds and open spaces. May it always be so.

Juvenile and Adult Sandhill Cranes

Introduction

In the heart of Fairbanks, Alaska, an oasis is held in trust for residents and travelers alike. Creamer's Field Migratory Waterfowl Refuge, an expanse of farm fields ringed by forested lands, provides a quiet place to walk, ski, or simply enjoy lunch. Surrounded by businesses, housing developments, and a four-lane highway, this three-square-mile remnant of farmland, complete with a quaint turn-of-the-century farmhouse and two handsome barns, has somehow escaped urbanization. The fields are gently rolling and free of permafrost, making them ideal for urban development. Instead, geese, ducks, and Lesser Sandhill Cranes by the thousands make use of the fields each spring and fall. And in winter, the land is a mecca for area dog mushers and skiers. What is the history behind the homey farmhouse and the Midwestern-style barns? And how is it that this farm gained refuge status?

Ask around, and an intriguing story unfolds of a pioneer farm built in the midst of an ancient flyway for cranes and waterfowl, and the townspeople who grew to appreciate the green fields and the birds that congregate there. When the farm eventually faced foreclosure, the farmer hoped to keep the land undivided for the benefit of the birds. The community, too, felt this connection to the land and was inspired to work with the farmer to save the farm from becoming just another housing complex or shopping mall. Together, they found a way to preserve Creamer's Field as a waterfowl refuge.

Under the management of the Alaska Department of Fish and Game (ADF&G), the refuge offers waterfowl protection, recreational access, environmental education, and opportunities for wildlife research. One less tangible but clearly evident aspect of the refuge is the appreciation or sense of place that so many people feel for it.

Sense of place can be described as a strong connection to a specific location that may define or strengthen one's self-identity. Sense of place incorporates beliefs, values, and feelings associated with a location. Knowing the history of a place can enhance one's connection to that place. For this reason, to truly appreciate this treasure we now call Creamer's Field Migratory Waterfowl Refuge, it is helpful to know the history of Creamer's Dairy and how it became a place for the birds.

Jessica A. Shepherd, M.A.
Fall 2025

Trumpeter Swan

Chapter One

Natural History of the Tanana Valley

Because of their antiquity, cranes have borne witness to Alaska's gradual transformation from arid grasslands to a region of vast forests and wetlands. For some nine million years, judging by a fossilized leg bone found in Nebraska, Lesser Sandhill Cranes have inhabited the North American continent, flying over a landscape that has changed profoundly over time. They have adapted to these changes and survived, even flourished, while somehow retaining their primordial elegance.

Change Over Time in Interior Alaska

The Tanana Valley is a 600-mile-long river drainage lying between the Yukon-Tanana Uplands to the north and the Alaska Range to the south. Forming near the border of Canada's Yukon Territory, the Tanana River runs westward across the State of Alaska before merging with the Yukon

River. It is the Yukon River's largest tributary within the State of Alaska. Fed by glaciers, snowmelt, and rain, the river is gray with silt, and its banks are crumbling and unstable.

As recently as 10,000 years ago, grassland dominated the whole of Alaska. Animals now extinct or found only on other continents inhabited the treeless, open plains. Interior Alaska remained ice-free during the last glacial period (20,000 to 100,000 years ago), and the climate was dry, with little rain and snowfall. There were few lakes, and salmon did not surge up the rivers in great numbers. Grasses, sedges, and sage comprised the majority of the plant species. Animals of this time period included camels and horses. Woolly mammoths roamed the valley floor, and lions waited out the heat of the day in grassy depressions.

Around 12,000 years ago, the global climate began to change. In Alaska, cloudy skies reduced evaporation while an increase in rainfall raised the levels of lakes and rivers. Streams with high silt loads were diluted with fresh water and snowmelt, resulting in increased fish populations. The swelling rivers and wetter climate led to an increase in willows, which quickly spread along drainages. As the glaciers melted in Canada and elsewhere, birch, aspen, and white and black spruce migrated northward and took hold. By 9,000 years ago, a woodland dominated by spruce trees defined Alaska's interior. This forest extends east across Canada and west into Siberia, creating a radius of trees around the circumpolar north called the Taiga or Boreal Forest.

Animal populations increased due to the change in climate and vegetation. Migratory bird numbers rose in response to a surge in insect populations and suitable nesting habitats. Moose, which were prevalent in the Interior 35,000 years ago, once again made their way into the Tanana Valley where willows, their favorite food source, now grew in profusion. Bison and elk also populated the Interior. And, possibly in response to this increase in wildlife, the first human inhabitants to settle in Alaska began making their way east across the Bering Strait and up the river drainages.

Native Vegetation

Present-day interior Alaska is a mosaic of white birch stands, shimmering aspen, tall white spruce, stunted black spruce, marshlands, and burn areas reseeded in hot-pink fireweed. The difference from one location to the next can be attributed to a number of variables. In general, low lying areas have poor drainage and are dotted with bogs and ponds. Permafrost is often just 12 to 30 inches below the surface. These cold soils are vegetated by black spruce and shrub species like willow and dwarf birch, with intermittent paper birch. Fire and cultivation can expose bare soils to solar radiation and result in lowering permafrost levels to four feet or more below the soil surface. Soils underlain with alluvial gravel, like those found at Creamer's Field, generally have adequate drainage and can support grain crops and other forms of agriculture.

Upland slopes generally have good drainage, and permafrost may not be present or may lie several feet deep—too deep to impact tree growth. These sites are typically forested with white spruce, birch, and aspen. However, on north-facing slopes, where the sun does not warm the soils adequately, permafrost typically dominates with a corresponding growth of black spruce and alder. In these forested regions, moss covers the forest floor in a spongy, continuous carpet. This moss provides an insulating layer over the permafrost, keeping it from thawing more than an inch or two during the warm days of summer. Open grasslands are not typically part of the Interior ecosystem. Any open field is likely the result of an oxbow that has separated from a river and, over time, filled in with rushes and grasses during its transition back to forest.

Climate

Interior Alaska is well known for its extreme winters. Temperatures of zero to -20 degrees Fahrenheit are the norm for December and January, and lows of -40 and even colder are not uncommon, occurring on an average of five days each winter as of 2024, down from an average of 14 days just 20 years earlier. While snow can occur anytime from September until June, October through March are the snowiest months. Winter temperatures typically dip below freezing during October. In the past, temperatures seldom broke freezing before April, with snow accumulating throughout the winter to an average snow depth of three feet a year. Based on 95 years of weather data, climate trends indicate an increase of three degrees in annual temperatures in the Fairbanks area between 1930 and 2025, with an average of 11 fewer days of recorded temperatures below -30 in the winter, and in the summer, an additional 32 days of above-freezing temperatures.

Sunlight in the winter months dwindles to less than four hours a day in late December. While the winter months are not generally cloudy, ice fog can prevail during periods of extreme cold. Ice fog, lasting for several days or even weeks at a time, occurs when cold air settles into the lowlands, water vapor rises from open leads of water or from home heating and car exhaust, and then freezes—staying suspended in the air until the inversion breaks.

Summer months are noteworthy for their perpetual daylight and warm temperatures. Interior Alaska is bathed in light continuously from early May until the first weeks of August, when dusk and then nightfall return. Temperatures in July typically register between a low of 52 degrees and a high of 73 degrees. However, temperatures in the 80s are not uncommon in June or July, with a few additional days of 90-degree temperatures.*

Total annual precipitation in the Interior averages 11.67 inches a year as of 2024 (an increase of two inches since precipitation measurements began in 1901). Most of the moisture falls during the summer months, with July averaging 2.26 inches of rain, followed by August with 2.10 inches. April is generally the driest month, with 0.34 inches of precipitation as rain or snow.

On average, April 27 is now the last date for freezing temperatures (compared to May 16 in the 1980s), and the growing season for crops and home gardens gets underway shortly thereafter. While frost can occur at any point during the summer, as of 2024, September 18 is currently the average date for the first killing frost (an advance of 19 additional growing days since 1989). This gives interior Alaska a growing season of about 144 days (a gain of 38 days in the past 35 years). With the abundance of daylight during this period, leafy vegetables such as lettuce, cabbage, peas, and broccoli grow rapidly. Grain crops, including barley and oats, flourish under these conditions as well, and, short of any extreme weather before a September harvest, the yield per acre can be respectable.

---

* See Appendix A: Fairbanks Alaska, Average Annual High and Low Temperatures, Precipitation, and Snowfall.

Interior Rivers

In the heart of Alaska's interior, the Chena River wanders down from the Tanana Uplands, fed by springs and runoff. The Chena runs clear but dark—stained a tea-brown by leaf tannins. It supports grayling and salmon in the summer and burbot after freeze-up in the fall. For much of its length, the Chena is deep enough to float a canoe, and toward its terminus, it can accommodate passing sternwheelers with waving tourists. Where the Chena and the Tanana Rivers wed, a swirling channel of clear water runs side-by-side with silty glacial meltwaters.

By late October, most Interior rivers freeze over. Come the end of March, the ice will be three feet deep or more. Underneath the ice, cold water still flows. Sometimes, this subsurface river encounters an ice dam where the water has frozen to the bottom. The river then finds a crack, allowing it to surge out over the surface of the existing ice. The overflow freezes upon exposure to frigid air temperatures, staining the white surface golden-brown from tannin-laden waters.

In late spring, the ice moans and creaks. Breakup can be dramatic, with a roaring, grinding sound as the water underneath surges forward and huge cubes of ice break loose and are squeezed up and out into a jumble of blue blocks. In other years, breakup is easy—the ice rots out from the bottom up and the top down until pockets of open water appear. Day by day, the sun and flowing water eat away at the shoreline ice until the ice is gone and the muddy banks begin caving into the flowing channel in the ever-changing gain and loss of silt along the shores of the Chena and Tanana Rivers.

Sandhill Cranes

Against a backdrop of late-winter trees, a pair of Lesser Sandhill Cranes flies westward, following a line of budding willows and a stream burbling with meltwater. Farm fields come into view, and the birds begin to descend. On the fields, plows have scraped the snow away in long rows to expose the soil, and volunteers have spread grain in readiness for the birds. Weary from weeks of flight, the pair circles, calling back and forth to each other. Their reedy cries are answered by other birds who have already arrived, and with deep strokes of gray wings, they slow their flight, swing down long, slender legs, and prepare to land. Here, on these protected fields, they will recover from their three-thousand-mile journey.

The Lesser Sandhill Crane is an annual favorite among area residents. The local Fairbanks population is just one of several varieties of Sandhills found throughout North America. The Sandhills breeding in the Lower Tanana

Sandhill Cranes in flight. Photograph by Ken Whitten.

Valley are intermediate in body size, and migrate north each spring from their wintering grounds in Texas. In late March, on the first leg of their migration, they join the annual aggregation of the mid-continent's migratory Sandhills at the Platte River in Nebraska. In the early 2020s, more than a million Sandhills were sighted.

Fairbanks Sandhills arrive at Creamer's Field Migratory Waterfowl Refuge around April 22, two weeks or more after the first Canada Geese and Trumpeter Swans arrive. Soon, the fields at the refuge, still half covered by snow, contain hundreds of the elegant gray birds, along with thousands of geese and ducks. Weary from their journey, the Cranes fatten up on grain, voles, and tubers as they wait for their nesting sites to melt free of snow. Here too, they engage in the wild, showy dances for which they are known.

Once the snow recedes, they fan out over the Lower Tanana Valley and Minto Flats to their nesting sites where they produce eggs, usually two, in a shallow nest of grass and sedges. In early June, after a month-long incubation,

A mature Sandhill Crane calling. Photograph by Ken Whitten.

precocial colts, covered in yellow down, hatch into a world of abundant insects and unending daylight. Come mid-August, the colts are as large as their parents and capable of flight.

In late August, the cranes once again congregate to feed and dance at Creamer's Field Migratory Waterfowl Refuge in preparation for their fall migration. The colts are distinguished from the adults by their high, thin peeping and lack of red crown. Around 3,000 cranes make this fall stopover at the Creamer's Field before continuing south at the beginning of September. Their journey will take them east over golden aspen forests and mountains capped with new snow, and south past sagebrush-covered slopes and vast grasslands to the open ranch lands, farms, and wildlife refuges in central Texas.

Yellow Warbler

Northern Pintails

Chapter Two

Early Contact and the Founding of Fairbanks

The Yukon River was the primary route of travel for early European fur seekers. The Russians established trading posts along the river during the late 1700s, followed by the British in the mid-1800s. The Tanana Valley, however, was little known by outside explorers until near the end of the nineteenth century. The first known exploration of the Tanana occurred in the mid-1870s when traders Arthur Harper and a gentleman known only as Bates traveled from the present location of Dot Lake, down the Tanana River to the Yukon. In 1885, Lieutenant Henry T. Allen, United States Cavalry members, and four crewmembers made the first study of the Tanana River drainage. Allen and his men set out in early March from the mouth of the Copper River and traveled 300 miles north up the Copper River before turning west to float down the Tanana to the Yukon and subsequently to the Koyukuk River—1,500 miles all told.

It was an epic journey, and the men nearly starved before reaching the Yukon River. Despite their hardships, Allen made excellent notes, and his maps became the template for charts of these rivers until official surveys were made twelve years later.

In 1896, a United States geological expedition undertaken by J.E. Spurr, H.B. Goodrich, and F.C. Schrader indicated probable gold deposits along tributaries to the Yukon, including the Fortymile River and Birch Creek, and they publicly speculated about gold in the Tanana Valley. Consequently, in 1898, two steamboats, the *Tanana Chief* and the *Potlatch*, made what was probably the first steam-powered trip up the Chena Slough. On board were 18 prospectors ready to take up pick and shovel amid the hills above the remote valley. The first significant gold discovery in the Tanana Valley occurred just after the turn of the century, and the story of this discovery became a local legend.

The Discovery of Gold and the Birth of a City

Felix Pedro, or Felice Pedroni in his native Italian, was the youngest of six children. Raised in a small village in northern Italy where his father found employment as a coal miner, Felix never learned to read or write and initially followed in his father's footsteps to work in the mines. But in 1881, at the age of 23, he set out for America. He found his way first to Carbonado, Washington, where he mined gold for several years before heading north to the Klondike gold fields. Here he tried his hand at gold mining until the late 1890s when he made his way west into Alaska. As luck would have it, Felix found and then lost a gold-rich creek near the Chatanika River north of Fairbanks.

He found work in the Circle City mines, but when his finances allowed, he stocked up on supplies and walked the 160 miles back to the Chatanika area. Time and again, he returned to search for the rich gold deposit he had lost, working with stubborn determination.

In late August of 1901, Felix and his mining partner, Tom Gilmore from Iowa, worked the hills north of the Chena Slough. They had exhausted their food supplies and subsisted on berries and wild game while contemplating the long walk to Circle City for resupply. On August 26, Felix and Tom caught sight of the smoke from a steamship several miles away on the Tanana River. They watched with interest as the ship attempted the Bates Rapids a few miles above the Chena Slough confluence. Boat captains typically considered the Bates Rapids to be the terminus of river navigation on the Tanana, as the river became too shallow for a boat bearing cargo. After several failed attempts to proceed up the Tanana by this route, the steamship headed back downriver and then turned to travel several miles up the Chena Slough. Felix and Tom, hoping for a quick remedy to their food shortage, made a beeline toward the ship.

The ship's captain, Charles Adams, having failed to find a way around the troublesome rapids on the Tanana River, probed his way up the Chena Slough but again ran into shallow waters. His next option was to unburden the boat of its passengers and cargo, having brought them as close to their destination as possible. E.T. Barnette and his wife Isabelle, along with a handful of helpers, had booked passage on the *Lavelle Young* from St. Michael and carried 130 tons of supplies—enough to open a trading post at Tanana Crossing many river miles further upstream.

Barnette, displeased at being deposited with his wares in this remote and uninhabited location so late in the year, attempted to persuade Captain Adams to take them back to the mouth of the Chena, where a small trading post had recently been established. The captain, however, expressed his concern about the difficulties he would encounter if he ran aground while moving downstream with a loaded boat. After a heated and emotional argument, with the refined Isabelle likely distraught at the turn of events, Barnette and Adams worked out a compromise. The captain agreed to take them downstream to a high bank on the south side of the slough, which Barnette had noticed on their way up. Here, Adams deposited his passengers along with enough supplies to outfit a small regiment. Pedro and Gilmore, upon reaching the stockpile of goods, became the first customers to load up on flour, bacon, and beans before heading back into the hills.

Barnette established a temporary trading post on the river and called his tiny enclave Chenoa City. He still intended to transfer his goods to Tanana Crossing the following summer; there, he planned to profit from a trail being built between the small coastal town of Valdez and the community of Eagle on the Yukon. For the time being, he and his wife and their workmen would have to overwinter on the banks of the Chena. He traded with Athabascans in the area and sold goods to a handful of miners. Things looked bleak for the Barnettes as winter's darkness and cold settled in, but their luck was about to change.

Eleven months later, in July of 1902, Felix Pedro worked alone. Tom Gilmore had headed back to Circle City. Although only 41, Felix had a weak heart, and the years of hard work had taken their toll. Nonetheless, he worked as best he could and found enough promising color to keep him in supplies. On or about July 22, 1902, he was working a small creek about 16 miles from the Chena Slough when he made a significant strike. He was too weak to sink the hole deep enough to hit bedrock, so he headed to Fairbanks for help. With the assistance of willing laborers, the strike's wealth was confirmed. The creek became known as Pedro Creek and the hill above it as Pedro Dome.

Claims were quickly staked on Pedro, Cleary, Gold, and Twin Creeks, and by the time summer ended, more than 110 claims had been staked on a dozen creeks throughout the surrounding area. A town began to grow out of the wilderness. Trees up and down the valley were felled for cabins and heat, and single-track roads were built out to the mining camps. Acting on the suggestion of Judge James Wickersham, Barnette named the growing community Fairbanks after Senator Charles Fairbanks of Indiana. (Senator Fairbanks later served as vice president under President Theodore Roosevelt.) In return, Judge Wickersham helped the community prosper by relocating his courthouse from Eagle to Fairbanks. Soon, a post office and a bank sprang up, and in 1903 the Northern Commercial Company (NC Company), a large retail chain, bought out the Barnette's log trading post.

Moose in Winter

Canada Geese and Trumpter Swans

Chapter Three

Two Families Settle in Fairbanks

Fairbanks was destined to grow into something more than just a tent town for miners as business-minded people constructed shops and built churches and schools in this remote but promising community in the north. Add to that the agricultural potential of the Tanana Valley, which intrigued farmers and herdsmen who read about it in papers across the nation. Two such families, the Hinckleys and the Creamers, tried their luck in several boom-and-bust towns before settling at last in Fairbanks, where they prospered.

The Creamers

Charles Newton Creamer, known as C.N., worked as a teamster for Wells Fargo Bank, driving the Weaverville stagecoach in the prosperous northern California mining town. C.N. and his wife, Mary Jane Todd Creamer, or Minnie, had seven children. Their son, Charlie, born in

Weaverville on May 4, 1889, was the only boy in the family. His sisters, from oldest to youngest, were Tessie, Mattie, Frances, Camellia, Genevieve, and Marian. In 1896, C.N.'s sister Emma and her husband Al Noyes came from Colorado for a visit. Emma and Al were fired up about their impending move to Juneau, a bustling gold-mining town where high-paying jobs were begging to be filled. Their enthusiasm was contagious, and when they headed north for Alaska, C.N. went with them.

Not long after they reached Juneau, they heard talk of a big gold strike in Dawson City, Canada, and they formulated a new plan. While Emma remained in Juneau, C.N. and Al made a trip to Seattle for six sturdy horses and then returned north to Dyea, near Skagway—the jumping-off point to the Dawson gold fields. In June of 1897, they set up business freighting goods from the beach in Dyea to Sheep Camp at the base of the Chilkoot Pass for miners en route to Dawson City, Canada. Once they unloaded the freight, it was up to the miners to haul the goods over the pass. Trip after trip, the miners would haul tremendous loads on their backs up the pass using steps cut into the ice.

From there, the miners would walk to Lake Bennett in British Columbia, Canada, construct a boat or raft, and begin the long float down to the Yukon River and on to Dawson City. C.N. and Al hauled freight day after day and watched the steady line of gold seekers as they made their way up and over the pass. Surely, they must have talked of throwing in their lot with the rest and heading to Dawson City.

In the spring of 1897, Minnie Creamer decided to join her husband and packed up the family home in Weaverville. She sailed to Juneau with her children, including Charlie, who had just turned nine, and remained there until

Thanksgiving Day when they made the short trip up to Dyea. After a difficult landing on the beach, Minnie found that the cabin C.N. had promised to have ready was no more than a tent, and the Thanksgiving dinner he'd prepared was, as Charlie recalled, "a big pot of sow bellies and beans." Eventually, C.N. built a two-story log house in Dyea for his family, and they remained there for two years while C.N. and Al ran the freighting business. The men had three two-horse teams, and young Charlie drove a team when they were shorthanded.

Not everyone who set out for the Dawson gold fields completed the trip. Jefferson Randolph "Soapy" Smith ran a shady gambling ring and swindled many would-be miners out of their grubstake money so that they returned to Dyea and headed home before they even began. Charlie remembered Soapy and how he dressed in a smart suit, not in the work clothes of the stampeders. Soapy and his gang of hotheads were involved in a shoot-out one night when irate townsfolk attempted to drive them out of Skagway. Soapy was killed in the volley of gunfire. This occurred in 1898, shortly before completion of the White Pass and Yukon Railway. Later, when Charlie lived in Fairbanks, he recognized three of the men in Soapy's gang. Some of them remained in Fairbanks for the rest of their lives, but they weren't gamblers anymore, and Charlie never revealed their identity.

The Creamer family faced multiple tragedies in 1899. Al, who had not seen his wife in nearly two years, arranged to travel to Juneau for a visit. Minnie sewed greenbacks (government currency backed by gold) into the lining of his coat and vest so that he could discretely transport the money, and he booked passage on the *Clara Nevada*. The boat was loaded with gunpowder, and according to regulations, she should have been unloaded at Berner's Bay before taking on passengers. But she steamed into Skagway first and picked up 60 passengers, including Al Noyes. As the boat entered Berner's Bay, it exploded, and all on board were killed. Al's body was never recovered. Shortly thereafter, the White Pass and Yukon Railway from Dyea to Sheep Camp was completed, and was out of a job. To add to the family's troubles, Tessie (C.N. and Minnie's oldest daughter) fell and injured her hip. The family went to Tacoma to seek medical treatment for her, but Tessie died of her injury.

In 1900, C.N. once again headed north, this time making the arduous trip from Tacoma to Dawson City to find work. In 1903, hearing rumors about the gold strikes in the Tanana Valley, he joined Fred Noyes (brother to Al Noyes) and headed to Fairbanks.

Finding the situation favorable, C.N. sent for Minnie and the children in the spring of 1904. The family traveled once again from Washington State to Skagway, and this time, they took the White Pass and Yukon Railway to Whitehorse, Canada. From Whitehorse, they traveled down the broad Yukon River to Dawson City on the *Selkirk* and then rode the *Sarah* to the Tanana River. Changing boats again, they traveled up the Tanana River to the Chena River on the *Tanana*. The steamship tied up in front of the NC Company, formerly E.T. Barnette's trading post, and young Charlie and his family had their first look at Fairbanks. "Everything was wide open," with saloons, gambling parlors, and dance halls, Charlie remembered many years later. The town consisted of only a few log cabins but no shortage of tents. Once again, Minnie and her children had come north to a bustling tent city.

Anna Carr and the Hinckleys

Meanwhile, in a similar fashion, another family embarked on a journey that would eventually lead them to Fairbanks. Charles T. Hinckley was born in Illinois and worked at the Hines pickle factory before making his way to Washington sometime around the turn of the century. He met and married Anniebelle "Belle" Carr, and together, they managed a dairy in Portland, Oregon. But newspaper stories of fortunes made from the gold fields to the north implied that a dairyman in the gold rush town of Nome could sell fresh milk for $5 a quart. The Hinckleys seized on the opportunity and departed Seattle aboard the *Nome City* schooner on June 7, 1900, with several cows in tow. They milked the cows twice each day aboard ship and sold the milk to pay for their passage. Four weeks later, they arrived in Nome, a tent city of 20,000 people on the sandy shores of the Bering Sea.

For eighteen months, they worked to establish a dairy, but life in Nome proved challenging. In September, as storms swept in from across the Pacific, the Hinckleys' tents were blown down by 75-mile-per-hour winds. With no trees for a log barn, the Hinckleys struggled to make do with double-walled tents to house the cows that first winter. Firewood was available, but only by making a 100-mile trip inland by dog team. To make matters worse, competition from several other dairymen brought the price of milk down to a dollar a quart.

In the fall of 1902, the Hinckleys returned to Washington, but come spring, they were back in Nome. They brought with them Belle's younger sister, Anastasia Elizabeth Carr. Born January 29, 1885, and known to everyone as Anna, she was a girl of eighteen. A spunky, petite brunette, she loved the trip north, with dancing and parties on the boat at night and church on Sundays.

In an undated memoir, she wrote:

> *I was a good sailor and enjoyed every minute of the trip. Even the huge ice pack we crept through for several days. … Then Nome at last. It was very dusty. I was disappointed. But the sea and the long beach were always clean, and we rode our horses there. I loved to sit and watch the waves come in. … In the winter the snow would almost cover the homes. Skiing was one of our main sports and we had our horses and cutter to drive and lots of parties.*

Anna found work at the Billy Rowe Boarding House, but she probably welcomed the news when her sister and brother-in-law began to consider a move. By the spring of 1904, the Nome gold rush had peaked, and it was time to look for new opportunities. The growing community of Fairbanks, located 1,280 miles inland by way of the Yukon and Tanana Rivers, would surely need fresh milk as news of the lucrative gold rush there spread.

The Hinckleys would have heard reports of good agricultural land in Alaska's interior. The Department of Agriculture published findings in 1901, stating, "It is chiefly the vast interior which will furnish the agricultural land in Alaska." The Tanana Valley purportedly had a longer window between frost dates than anywhere along the Yukon River drainage. In addition, the Homestead Act, which had been extended to Alaska in 1898, was amended in 1902, allowing homesteaders to lay claim on 320 acres, double the 160 acres granted throughout the rest of the country.

The discovery of a rich gold deposit near an area of agricultural promise truly set Fairbanks apart from other gold-mining towns, suggesting longevity beyond the initial flush of wealth that gold provided.

Anna joined the Hinckleys as they, along with three cows and their best horse, headed to Fairbanks on the first boat of the season. The cows helped to offset the cost of their passage, providing fresh milk for the crew and passengers.

In her memoir, Anna wrote of a beautiful trip:

> *The trees and all nature so green, after the barren beaches of Nome. We had fresh vegetables and game picked up at trading posts where we stopped to get wood for the boat.*

After 27 days, a small cluster of log buildings and tents came into view. Fairbanks at last. Anna and the Hinckleys steamed into Fairbanks in July 1904. Anna was 19 that summer while Charlie Creamer was a tall, gangly boy of 15. Their paths would cross constantly in tiny Fairbanks over the next several years.

Bohemian Waxwings

Red-breasted Nuthatch

Sandhill Crane

Chapter Four

Establishing a Dairy in Early Fairbanks

The Hinckley and Creamer families settled into small log cabins not far from one another. The Hinckleys established a dairy on Fourth Avenue between Cowles and Kellum, and they cleared the land, cutting spruce trees to build a low log building. The cows wintered at one end of the building, and the family lived under the same roof at the other end. The dairy was located just two blocks west of the red-light district. "The Row" on Fourth Street, between Cushman and Barnette, had a tall wooden fence with a gate built across both ends of the street to screen the girls and their customers from the rest of the town folk. The town did not extend much farther than the dairy, and during an interview in 1959, Anna recalled riding her horse in Fairbanks "along trails through the trees, on what are now Cowles and Kellum Streets."

Anna Carr left the family dairy to marry Louis Golden on October 2, 1904, with Archdeacon Hudson Stuck

Original log dairy. Albert Johnson Photo Collection #89-166-101, 1905–1917, Hinckley's Dairy Archives, University of Alaska, Fairbanks.

presiding over the ceremony. Louis was a good deal older than Anna. He ran a saloon and dance hall and was something of a gambler. Anna did not care for his lifestyle and encouraged him to open a grocery instead. Together they established Golden's Grocery, located on First Avenue and Wickersham.

C.N. Creamer and Fred Noyes staked out property on the north side of the Chena Slough, across the water from Fairbanks. The property ran from Graehl Landing to the eastern end of a slough they named Noyes Slough. Fred established the Noyes Mill (later renamed the Tanana Mill) on the slough, and C.N. assisted Fred with the mill. In addition, C.N. operated a ferry to transport people to and from Fairbanks across the Chena Slough, and he also cut and sold ice from the slough in the winter. He had a two-story frame house built in Graehl (near the location of the present-day Wendell Street Bridge) and soon had 24 head of horses and mules. C.N. then established a business unloading freight from steamships at the mouth of the Chena and freighting it the six miles up to Fairbanks.

Young Charlie attended seventh grade at Main School that first year. The school had opened the year before and already had 50 students. He returned the next fall, but after a falling-out with the principal, he decided he'd had enough schooling. He found work at Waechter's Meat Market, where he helped drive cows from town out to Gilmore Trail in the spring. He remained with them throughout the summer before driving them back into town when it was time to slaughter them in the fall. Gilmore Trail, called Ridge Road at that time, was the first trail out to the gold mines. Come fall, Charlie and Ralph Waechter rode horseback to Circle on the Yukon River, collected a herd of cows brought up from Seattle, and drove the herd 160 miles into town. For extra income, Charlie often made home deliveries for Golden's Grocery, and as he matured into his tall, lanky frame, he became a "favorite with the ladies."

Fairbanks Agricultural Experiment Station

By 1905, Fairbanks had a population of 2,500, and the route to Valdez had improved to a wagon trail. The city's residents put up with muddy streets, but they soon enjoyed limited phone service and a 75-horsepower engine that provided enough electricity to power 1,000 lights. Those living outside the radius of electricity used kerosene lamps and candles to brighten the long winter nights. Construction began on the Tanana Mines Railway (later known as the Tanana Valley Railroad) with plans to lay track between the town of Chena on the Tanana and Fairbanks, and extending to the mines in Fox, Olnes, Gilmore City, and Chatanika at the terminus. This greatly facilitated mining operations as heavy equipment could be brought in.

In addition to a lucrative mining industry, the Tanana Valley saw an increase in agricultural efforts with 82 registered homesteads in 1905. With hopes of gaining insight into farming in the challenging north, Fairbanks residents sent a petition to the Secretary of Agriculture requesting the establishment of an agricultural experiment station in the Tanana Valley. In response, Charles C. Georgeson, special agent in charge of the United States Agricultural Experiment Stations, arrived at the end of July and spent the first few days of his visit traveling on horseback to different homesteads to ascertain the region's agricultural potential.

Under the directive from the Secretary of Agriculture, Georgeson had already established experimental stations in Sitka, Kodiak, Rampart Village, and Copper Center. He found the soils in the Tanana Valley to be nearly free of rocks and easy to work once the trees were cleared away. Local gardeners simply amended the loam soil with manure and reaped impressive results. Satisfied by what he saw, Georgeson set about locating a site for an agricultural experiment station.

Georgeson first considered the Delta Junction area because large tracts of land remained available. Locating the experimental station near Fairbanks, however, would benefit a greater number of people. The Fairbanks Chamber of Commerce, not wanting to miss this opportunity, used its powers of persuasion to interest Georgeson in a 1,394-acre tract of land between the communities of Chena and Fairbanks. The tract was situated on a south-facing slope, making it well suited for cultivation. Moreover, the location was adjacent to the Tanana Mines Railroad, thus providing good access to the community.

The site proved to be quite satisfactory, and by 1906, a wide assortment of garden crops grew in neat fields. Georgeson also grew an assortment of flowers, adding to the visual appeal. The Fairbanks community took note of the crops and techniques that produced results and incorporated what they found to produce bountiful home gardens and field crops.*

Fairbanks Business District Burns

Before the first garden rows were planted in the spring of 1906, Fairbanks faced near ruin. On the evening of May 22, young Charlie sat in the barbershop getting a shave and a haircut while a few doors down, Dr. Moore, a dentist in the Fairbanks Building on Cushman Street, attended to a patient. An alcohol lamp used to sterilize the doctor's instruments stood burning below an open window. Suddenly, a breeze puffed out the curtain and the fabric passed over the flame. In seconds, the room was afire, and with frightening speed, the flames advanced until the three-story building was ablaze. Fortunately, Dr. Moore and his patient were able to run from the building, alerting others as they fled. But unusually dry spring weather and the closely spaced wood buildings proved a recipe for disaster.

In minutes, much of downtown Fairbanks was in flames. The firemen's hand-drawn carts were no match

---

* Two other field stations in Alaska followed: The Matanuska Farm Station began operations in 1914, and the Palmer Research Center opened in 1948. These three stations continue to operate, while all earlier stations shut down during or shortly after the Depression. In 1991, the Fairbanks Agricultural Experiment Station became the Fairbanks Research Station, retaining a research garden, 260 acres of crops, and a 50-acre research forest. The garden, now called the Georgeson Botanical Garden, is open to visitors and area gardeners who walk among a dazzling display of flowers, fruits, and vegetables and glean information for boosting home garden productivity. The research station and garden are under the management of the University of Alaska Fairbanks.

for the inferno, and water pressure soon ran low. The Washington-Alaska Bank, the jail, the Riverside Hotel, and the Senate Saloon were engulfed in flames. Only quick thinking saved the rest of the town. When extra water pressure was needed for the fire hoses, the manager at the NC Company called for all the stores of bacon to be thrown into the boiler. The 2,000 pounds of sizzling bacon raised the water pressure enough to contain the blaze. The fire had consumed everything from First Avenue to Third and from Cushman Street to Lacey. The entire business district had burned except for the NC Company warehouses. Yet the townsfolk of Fairbanks were not to be deterred. Rumor has it that the sounds of saws and hammers could be heard even before the smoke cleared.

The Hinckleys Expand the Dairy in Fairbanks

Perhaps inspired by the rebuilding going on around them, the Hinckleys bought out the Morton and Downing Dairy on the north side of the Chena Slough in the community of Graehl. When they moved their business to this location, they constructed a log barn and a two-story log house. They acquired 14 milk cows and sold milk for one dollar a quart. They expanded their customer base, but shipping milk bottles from Seattle proved beyond their means. Instead, they improvised and used "imperial quart" wine bottles. These green wine bottles, filled with cool, rich milk and sealed with a cork, were delivered to homes and restaurants throughout the Fairbanks area using wagons. In the winter, the dairy delivered milk by horse-drawn sleigh. Charles Hinckley fitted the sleigh with a small shed containing a wood-burning stove to keep the bottles from freezing. Merwin "Buster" Anderson, raised by his grandparents C.N. and Minnie, was a small child when the Hinckleys ran the dairy in the community of Graehl. He remembered going along on the three-hour milk route many times.

According to Buster, Mr. Hinckley was "a very jolly person, a hard worker, but a happy man. Mrs. Hinckley did the milking and all the cooking." Young Charlie Creamer also helped with milk delivery from time to time, and he met the old miner Felix Pedro and his wife Mary when he delivered milk to their house on Clay Street.

In 1910, the Hinckleys purchased 327.42 acres of land a mile west of town on Ester Road (later called College Road). A notarized deed states that Charles Hinckley purchased the land from E.G. Murray. The selling price, however, is unknown. The land at the time of purchase contained improvements that included a cabin, a barn, fencing, and a ditch. The farm had upwards of 46 acres of open grassland called Murray's Meadow. Mr. Murray may have cleared the land for grazing, or the meadow may have been the remnant of an old river channel.

The Hinckleys built a barn on the land with logs cut from the surrounding woods. Moss pressed between the logs and a two-foot-thick sod roof provided protection against the weather. Mr. Hinckley used the barn in the summer months for twice-daily milking and storage. For several years, he drove the cows out to the homestead to graze in the spring and summer and herded them back toward town in September to overwinter in Graehl. He tilled the open land and grew wheat, oats, peas, and barley for winter feed, supplementing what he grew with shipments of hay and grain from Seattle. Feeding cattle through the winter represented a significant expense; feed shipped from Seattle cost $165 a ton, and each cow required three tons of feed to get through the winter. The Hinckleys also faced the challenge of keeping good workers since each rumor of a new gold strike was an enticement to grab a shovel and head to the creeks.

Gold contributed significantly to the city's economic growth. In 1903, gold production amounted to just $40,000. In 1904, that figure rose to $600,000. The gold assayed in 1906 amounted to $9 million and rose to $30 million in 1910. In terms of production, the value of gold extracted in Fairbanks surpassed both the Klondike and Nome strikes. The continued increase in production drew a steady stream of settlers during the years before the First World War. While many folks came intending to work in the gold mines, others came to offer their services, be it as doctors, storekeepers, or preachers. In 1909, some 3,000 people lived within the city of Fairbanks with many more scattered throughout the hills. The town had schools, churches, saloons, two breweries, three sawmills, and two machine shops. The NC Company ran steam heat to nearby businesses and homes. Dances and socials were held on a regular basis, and one did not have to look far for warmth and entertainment.

Wood was the only source of heat in the growing community, and by 1913, the city burned 12,000–14,000 cords of wood annually. Trees were cut for miles around until the hills in every direction were bare. The sawmill Fred Noyes had built in 1904 prospered, and in 1910, he moved the operation to Illinois Street (the current site of the Golden Valley Electric Company). He had a stately home built on Illinois Street with finely crafted furniture shipped from England all the way around Cape Horn. (The home still stands today in quiet elegance.) That same year, he built a 60-foot stern-wheeler, The *Idler*, which he used for recreation. By the 1920s, Fred had become one of the wealthiest men in the Alaska Territory.

New modes of transportation made headway in Interior Alaska, hinting at great changes for the future. The first automobile rolled down the streets in 1906, and by 1914, there were 25 automobiles in town. Then construction began for a college west of the city, adjacent to the Fairbanks Agricultural Experiment Station. Judge James Wickersham placed the cornerstone on July 4, 1915. Perhaps even more exciting was the impending construction of the Alaska Railroad, which would connect Fairbanks to the seaport town of Seward, 400 miles to the south. Fairbanks appeared to be on the fast track to economic growth and prosperity.

In 1915, the Hinckleys moved their operations entirely to the land on College Road. They disassembled their log home, numbering each log and moving it to the new home site. Once on location, they reassembled the logs and rebuilt the house. This house now serves as the Farmhouse Visitor Center at the Creamer's Field Migratory Waterfowl Refuge. The Hinckleys also built a new barn as the old one had begun to sink into the soft ground. This time, the logs for the barn had to be cut some 40 miles up the Chena River and floated down due to the lack of trees locally. The family's years of hard work were paying off. On February 10, 1917, court records proclaimed that "Charles Timothy Hinckley is granted ownership of 327 42/100 acres, having met the homestead requirements."

As the decade drew to a close, the prosperity the city had enjoyed during its early years faded, and Fairbanks experienced an economic downturn. In 1918, gold production in Alaska dropped off as World War I brought crippling inflation. With most mines unable to operate at a profit, people left in great numbers to enlist or find better jobs in the States. Charlie Creamer enlisted in the United States Army and was first stationed at Fort Gibbon, Alaska, where the Tanana and Yukon Rivers join, and then in Iowa for six months. He was discharged and returned to Fairbanks in 1918, where he soon found work with an Alaska Railroad construction crew.

Prohibition swept the nation, beginning in Alaska in 1918 by popular vote and continuing until 1933. However, Alaskans are known for their ingenuity, and many found ways around the law prohibiting the sale and consumption of alcohol. During that first dry winter, Charlie's friend Frank Miller kept six barrels of whiskey under the Isabelle Creek Bridge on the south edge of the dairy.

Bootleggers ran a still up the Salcha River, and Mike Yankovich, a potato farmer in the hills northwest of town (where the University of Alaska Large Animal Research Station is now), brewed some pretty good whiskey, according to Charlie. Mike would bring a wagonload of potatoes to town, hiding bottles of moonshine under the load. Even the Hinckleys found a way to make whiskey in a three-gallon milk can.

Anna and Charlie Leave Alaska and Marry

Anna's marriage to Louis Golden faltered, and having no children, they divorced. Anna's parents still lived in Washington State and were now quite elderly. In 1918, at age 33, Anna returned to Washington to care for them. Few courtship details are known, but Charlie Creamer followed Anna to Washington two years later, leaving Fairbanks by train on September 19, 1920. Charlie and

Anna were married on October 16 of that same year in Seattle, Washington. Many years later, when asked about Anna's divorce from Louis Golden and Charlie's subsequent marriage to her, Charlie gave his warm laugh and stated, "When they split up, I fell heir to her." On March 11, 1922, Anna gave birth to Donald George (Don) Creamer in Pioneer, Washington, where Charlie and Anna had settled. He was to be their only child.

The Creamers ran a strawberry farm for a time, but Charlie did not care for the work. Instead, they invested in a chicken farm, which they ran for the next six years, selling chicks throughout southern Washington and around the Portland area. However, Charlie grew tired of the rainy winters and suggested a move back north. Anna liked Washington, so as a compromise, they planned a visit in May 1927. Charlie would look for work, and they would decide on a move at that point.

Moose in Summer

Adult Sandhill Cranes with Colt

Snow Geese

Chapter Five

Creamers Purchase and Modernize the Dairy

Anna and Charlie's 1927 trip from Seattle to Fairbanks was easier than in years past because the railroad from Seward to Fairbanks had been completed in 1923 after eight years of construction. With five-year-old Don along, Charlie and Anna boarded a boat from Seattle to Seward and then took a train from Seward to Fairbanks, overnighting in Curry en route. The trip took five days by boat followed by two days on the train.

Once they arrived in Fairbanks, they stayed with Charlie's parents, who lived on the 500 block of Graehl Street. It did not take long to see that Fairbanks had undergone favorable changes in the seven years they had been "Outside." Completion of the railroad provided a boost to the city's economy, which had been in a downward slump since the war. Before the railroad, people had ordered their food and goods a year in advance. Now, goods could be shipped from Seattle in ten days so produce and other items were available year-round. Trains also allowed for coal deliveries, alleviating concerns about a wood shortage for heating businesses and homes. In addition, the railroad facilitated the delivery of large mining dredges, which breathed new life into the gold industry.

The Fairbanks Exploration Company (FE Company), a subsidiary of the United States Smelting, Mining, and Refining Company, was in the process of establishing three gold dredging operations. They needed men to lay roads, build power plants, and operate electric equipment and dredges for the mining camps. The FE Company held the key to revitalizing the Fairbanks economy. Charlie inquired about a job and felt confident he would be hired the following spring, and Anna consented to the move.

In early September, the Creamers returned to Washington State where chicken prices had dropped to 15 cents a bird. They stayed through the winter and sold off everything they could. In late April 1928, they returned to Fairbanks, bringing 1,500 broilers, 500 hens, and 40 crates of eggs with them. At that time, fresh eggs and live chickens were still hard to obtain in Fairbanks during the winter. In the years before rail transportation, eggs were stored in a cool cellar all winter long and were turned regularly to prevent spoiling. The taste of the eggs grew stronger as the winter progressed so that by spring, the people of Fairbanks were most receptive to fresh eggs and eager for hens. The Creamers sold their first laying hens for four dollars apiece.

They stayed at the farm that summer with the Hinckleys. Charles Hinckley was 55 years old and had been a dairy farmer for more than thirty years. He had 12 milk-producing cows, and his wife, Belle, still milked them all, morning and night.

During the early 1900s, dairy farmers did all the milking, bottle washing, and processing by hand without the benefit of milking machines and sterilizers. Pasteurization had been developed in the early 1860s after Louis Pasteur, a French chemist, found that heating milk delayed spoilage and greatly reduced the spread of milk-born illnesses. But for small dairies such as the Hinckleys', investing in pasteurization equipment was cost prohibitive.

As early as the 1890s, scientists had determined that humans could contract bovine tuberculosis by drinking milk from infected cows. Further study indicated that cows confined together in barns for much of the winter had a much higher incidence of the disease than free-range dairy herds. In Alaska, a federally contracted veterinarian inspected farms twice a year. In August 1919, when examining the Hinckleys' stock, the veterinarian found that 25 of the 26 cows tested positive for bovine tuberculosis. The only means of eradicating the disease was to slaughter the cows. This done, the dairy ceased milk production on August 24, 1919, with the Hinckleys receiving some government compensation for their loss. Because the Hinckleys operated the only local dairy at the time, the city of Fairbanks went without milk for several weeks until new cows could be shipped up on a barge from the States.

The Hinckleys placed the dairy up for sale in November 1924 but so far no one had come up with the purchase price. The asking price of $12,000 included the log farmhouse and the low log barn, several smaller buildings, 12 milk-producing Holsteins, one Holstein bull, 12 calves, an assortment of dairy utensils and farming equipment, and all 327 acres. Charlie and Anna had likely decided to buy the dairy during their final winter in Washington. They received financing two weeks after returning to Fairbanks and closed on the purchase on May 1, 1928. Charlie had worked off and on for the Hinckleys for years. He knew the basics of dairy farming and was a hard worker. Anna could do the bookkeeping, and she had good business sense.

Charlie and Anna borrowed $2,000 from the First National Bank of Fairbanks where his sister Mattie's husband, Ed Stroecker, worked as a loan officer. Ed later became bank president. Then Charlie secured $6,000 in a private loan from Bill McGrath, a longtime Fairbanks miner. They paid the balance to the Hinckleys in installments over the next five years. The Hinckleys made their goodbyes and moved to Washington, where they opened a roadhouse between Olympia and Seattle. Anna was 43 and Charlie was 39 in 1928, the year they bought the farm. On August 21, 1933, the Hinckleys conveyed the land in full to the Creamers through the courts in Washington State.

The Creamers bought the farm just as agriculture began to take hold in Alaska. In 1930, there were 500 farms in the territory, up from 12 in 1900. All around Fairbanks, forests gave way to croplands and livestock. To the north of Creamer's Dairy, the aptly named Farmer's Loop Road became the farm belt for Fairbanks as homesteaders cleared the land section by section and planted potatoes and grains.

Building the Herd

Initially, Charlie had one hired man. Together they milked the cows by hand, strained the milk, and delivered it to area stores and restaurants. It took them about two hours each morning and two hours each evening to finish the milking. A quart of milk sold for 25 cents. In addition,

Charlie grew and harvested oats and peas for the cattle, built sheds, and mended equipment.

Charlie and Anna sought to expand the business, and just a month after buying the dairy, they bought out the Slater herd, which consisted of 10 milk cows, a yearling, and two calves. In the early 1930's, when Harry and Louisa Buzby, owners of Buzby's Dairy (on what is now Ladd Field Air Force Base) put their cattle up for sale, Charlie purchased the herd of 19 cows and walked them over the fields to College Road. Then, in 1937, Charlie added to his herd of Holsteins by purchasing 10 golden Guernsey cows, known for the high fat content in their milk.

The Creamers grew their herd as competing dairies folded. Initially, six or seven small dairies provided for the

Milking cows at Creamer's Dairy (circa 1930). Friends of Creamer's Field Photo Archives.

community's needs, but soon, only two dairies supplied the community—the Creamers' and the Bentleys'.

Henry T. Bentley began his dairy in 1912 and ran it with the help of his three sons. Born in England, he learned the restaurant trade as a youth and ran the Butte Restaurant in Fairbanks from 1903–1912. His dairy operation expanded, and before long, he was milking a dozen cows a day. In the fall of 1930, the Bentleys lost their barn (and apparently their livestock) to a fire. This resulted in a local milk shortage. Consequently, the Creamers purchased six cows from Washington and shipped them up by train to boost their milk production. The Bentleys then received an order of twelve milk cows in January of 1931 and rebuilt their barn in May, improving upon the old barn by adding a concrete foundation.

At first, the Creamers' farm had no electricity or running water. A well with a hand pump provided water for the cows. In the winter, Charlie and his farmhand William (Bill) Oskam, Sr. milked the cows and strained the frothy milk by lantern light.

As the business grew, Charlie and Anna hired more help. When they couldn't find workmen locally, they advertised through the Seattle newspapers. For a number of years, Leonard Neumann worked for the Creamers and made ice cream, and Oscar Canton, a native of Finland, was their maintenance man. Oscar was a little unusual. He chose to room in the attic, just under the roof, and without the benefit of insulation. He slept there for years and kept warm in the winter with a bearskin. He finally determined that he needed a Finnish wife and returned to Finland to find one. Oscar never returned to Fairbanks, and no one ever heard how his search turned out.

While the farm kept the Creamers remarkably busy, Anna never lacked for energy, and she loved to dance. She and Charlie often went out in the evening to socialize, Anna in a floral-print dress and mink coat, while Charlie sported a dapper hat and suit. Local dance halls offered live music, featuring a blend of big band, swing, and jazz.

She was "a real dynamo," according to her granddaughter Jeannie Creamer. Anna never seemed tired and didn't complain about the endless work. Moreover, she expected everyone else to work just as hard as she did. She oversaw all the cooking for the hired men and got up every morning by five to start the coffee and get breakfast on the table. Anna was a good cook and a "mother hen," according to Jeannie. She tended a large garden, raised chickens, and did the bookkeeping and banking, including applying for loans. In business correspondence, Anna took to signing her name "A.E. Creamer," and the return correspondence frequently addressed her as "Mr. A.E. Creamer," which did not bother her at all. She found time to be an active member of the Pioneer Women of Alaska. And on Sundays, Anna arrived at the Immaculate Conception Church promptly at nine with Don trailing behind her. Charlie did not attend church.

Don took to farm life and rode horses from an early age. When he was seven or eight, he tried to saddle up his horse for the first time. He got the saddle on all right and mounted the animal, but when the horse went around the corner of the barn, Don found himself, still in the saddle, hanging upside-down underneath the horse. He had not tightened the cinch sufficiently.

Although he had no brothers or sisters, Don grew up surrounded by family. Three of Charlie's sisters—Mattie, Marian, and Frances—remained in Fairbanks and were raising families of their own. Don's grandparents, C.N. and Minnie Creamer, continued to live in Fairbanks for the remainder of their lives.

Increasing Crop Production

As the farm prospered, Charlie invested much of his energy in raising crops to see his livestock through the winter. In the early 1930s, Charlie grew about 60 acres of feed annually, but when he lost the crop three years in a row due to rainy weather, he had to purchase feed from the NC Company at $120 a ton. Consequently, Charlie and Anna decided to switch to silage for their winter feed. The silage, a mixture of oats and peas, would heat up and ferment in the round silo towers and could be used throughout the winter to provide a nutrient-rich feed for the cows. The oats and peas did not need to be dried in the field but could be harvested and loaded directly into the silos, reducing problems associated with rainy weather. The Creamers grew oats and peas together in the field to make the silage. The oats supported the trailing pea vines so that a regular mowing machine could cut it and side rakes could load it. In 1934, the Creamers built two 100-ton silos and eventually replaced these with two 200-ton silos, seeking additional financing to build them. In addition, they grew barley for grain and brome grass for hay.

Every year, Charlie increased the size of his fields, cutting trees and pulling the stumps out of the black loam with horses. Along with a small crew, he grew feed for 30 milk cows, eight calves, eight horses, and 12 hogs. He cultivated the well-drained soil and left off clearing where the permafrost lay close to the surface, leaving the boggy forests for the fox and moose. In the 1940s, the

Creamers purchased additional land, eventually increasing their holding by another 377 acres, located mostly north of Farmer's Loop Road. This included the 320-acre Roy Shafer homestead that Charlie bought for $5,500 at a public auction on October 5, 1948.

At the end of each growing season, after the crops were put up for the year, Charlie culled the old stock from the herd. In the back of the hay shed, he shot the cows and hung them on a crossbeam to be skinned. Here the meat cured for a couple of days, with the cool fall weather keeping it fresh.

Adding Farming Equipment to the Dairy

As their milk sales to area restaurants and stores increased, Charlie and Anna retired the old delivery wagons and bought their first delivery vans around 1929. They began home-delivery routes in 1932 or 1933, about the same time that they started making ice cream. Charlie

Creamer's Dairy delivery truck, a 1935 Ford with a woodburning stove, parked in front of the Steel Hotel truck (circa 1936–1937). Don Creamer Collection. Friends of Creamer's Field Photo Archives.

fitted the vans with tiny wood stoves and smokestacks that rose out the back windows to keep the milk from freezing in the bottles during the winter. The driver laid the fire before leaving the warmth of the barn and then lit it when the van began to cool down around Second Avenue. After a few more stops, the driver adjusted the damper, which would usually suffice until he completed the route. In the summers, the delivery routes extended out to the mining camps, where the miners enjoyed ice cream after dinner with their coffee. Don often accompanied his father on the morning milk run before school. He helped on the route until 8:30 a.m., then ducked into the Imperial Cigar Store near the Co-Op Diner to read magazines until it was time for school. By the age of 11, he had learned to drive the Model A Ford delivery truck, and he took it out alone to make deliveries to the gold-mining camps of Ester and Chatanika.

Summer milk deliveries were done in the early years without the benefit of refrigeration. The driver wet gunnysacks and laid them over the milk cans to keep them cool. Charlie enjoyed telling the story of Frank Going. Going delivered milk and newspapers thirty miles out to the mining camps, driving out one day and coming back the next. In those days, milk came in three-gallon cans and drivers dispensed it with a quart measure. During a June 1973 interview, Charlie relayed, "Well, them days they had these little anchovies for a snack in the bar. And somebody dumped anchovies into his [Going's] milk can." So Going headed out the next morning, having stored his milk in the cool creek overnight. He arrived at the home of well-to-do jewelers, Mr. and Mrs. Sutter. When he poured out a quart of milk for them, "here came the fish." Going jumped back and said, "My God, the can got too deep in the river, I guess."

The purchase of new delivery vans foreshadowed the acquisition of new farm machinery, and in 1934, the Creamers bought their first gasoline-powered tractor. Horses required feed year-round, and the teamsters, who used to work ten- and twelve-hour days, now headed home after an eight-hour day due to Franklin D. Roosevelt's National Recovery Act, which established a maximum workweek of 40 hours. So, Charlie made the switch to tractors and bought a Case Model L in 1935. These early tractors did not completely replace horses because they frequently got stuck in the muddy fields. But by the 1940s, crawler tractors were available, and with their wide, continuous tread, they worked even in the snow. Charlie and Anna also added new farm equipment. In 1936, in addition to a second Case tractor, they purchased gangplows, brush-breaking plows, hay loaders, a disc harrow, and a side delivery rake.

A fire truck was the next addition to the growing fleet. Fire service did not extend outside of town in those days, and when a civil defense fire truck became available for a volunteer fire crew, Charlie agreed to house it. Subsequently, the dairy responded to most fires in the area, and Chuck Oster became the main driver. It had a good siren, but it did not go very fast, never exceeding 30 miles per hour, even going downhill.

Then, in the late 1930s or early 1940s, Charlie acquired a Detroit Chalmers convertible. This handsome car passed through several hands. Initially, it belonged to a Dr. Cassel. Charlie's uncle, Fred Noyes, bought it when the doctor moved away. Then, when Fred moved to the lower 48 states, C.N. acquired it. C.N. did not care to drive much, however, and told Charlie that if he wanted it, "he better come get it." Charlie eventually restored the Chalmers and gave it to Don.

Farmhouse and Dairy Improvements

By the early 1930s, the dairy was due for modernization. The green wine bottles were gone, replaced with thick glass milk bottles, but these were still washed by hand with a brush and set upside-down to dry. Charlie processed the milk by pouring it from the milking bucket through a strainer and into a 10-gallon can. The milk can was set to cool in a water tank and decanted into two gallon cans that were then used to fill the milk bottles. Charlie made ice cream with salt and ice that his father, C.N. Creamer, cut from the river in the winter. C.N. cut the ice with a handsaw into 200-pound blocks, about two feet square, and stored it, packed in sawdust, in the large icehouse by the Wendell Street Bridge. The ice usually lasted all summer.

With an eye toward modernizing, Anna and Charlie built a new milk house in 1934 and equipped it with a Baker ice machine to generate ice for ice cream. They added modern electric separators, a new refrigeration plant, and a new sterilizing room complete with a boiler to provide hot water and steam for washing bottles and cans. Bottle fillers sped up the decanting process, and milking machines relieved the men of hours of hand milking. "No effort is spared to make this dairy the most sanitary one in Alaska," according to a write-up in the local paper. The dairy now produced milk, cream, butter, ice cream, and cheese.

The summer of 1936 brought additional changes to the dairy. No sooner had the crops been planted than plans were underway for a series of construction projects. Anna and Charlie hired laborers to move the farmhouse several yards closer to the barns and onto a new root cellar with a cement foundation. Charlie oversaw the addition of a modern kitchen and bathroom on the north side of the farmhouse, and the house's exterior underwent a transformation when white siding was applied over the old log structure. A five-car garage became the next project.

In the fall of 1936, the dairy, purported to be the largest farm in Alaska under cultivation, produced 30 bushels of threshed barley per acre—a satisfactory yield even by Lower 48 standards. The Creamers and their crew raised 200 tons of oats and peas to provide for 40 milk cows, 16 calves, and five horses. The dairy shipped milk and other dairy products by truck, rail, and plane to Livengood, Circle, Nome, and Dawson City. The dairy's success came just as farmers throughout the central plains of the United States dealt with record heat, frightening dust storms, and widespread crop failure.

Although the Depression of the 1930s dragged on for much of the country, Alaska recovered much sooner, largely due to a surge in dredge mining operations. Because of President Roosevelt's decision in 1934 to increase the value of gold from $20 to $35 an ounce, the gold rush in and around Fairbanks rebounded, becoming the largest gold producer in the State at that time.

Construction of the First Louden Barn

Once the Creamers remodeled the house, the deterioration of the old log barn became strikingly evident. The floor and lower logs were rotting, and dairy operations were quickly outgrowing the limited space it offered. Consequently, in 1938, the Creamers contracted with the Louden Machinery Company in Iowa to build a large Iowa-style barn, so named because of the distinctive gothic-arch roof, which was common throughout Iowa. Workmen poured concrete footings to a height of three feet, and frame construction began on the barn walls for a building that would measure 110 feet long and 36 feet wide. The loft walls extended an additional 10 feet above the standard 32-foot height (for a total height of 42 feet) so it could hold 165 tons of hay—enough to feed 55 cows through the winter. The resulting structure had a curved metal roof and three gleaming ventilating cupolas on top.

The contractors installed a steam heater, blowers, and fans to provide ventilation and distribute heat evenly. The walls were a foot thick and insulated with sawdust, and after the first winter, the Creamers never used the steam heat because the cows provided enough warmth. Cork brick flooring eased the strain of confinement for the cows during the long winter months, and automatic water fountains quenched their thirst. A track ran down the center of the building for a cart to transport manure out of the barn. The barn was a state-of-the-art addition to the farm, and the $13,700 price tag for materials and labor surpassed the amount the Creamers had paid for the entire farm just ten

Louden barn and cows prior to 1947. Friends of Creamer's Field Photo Archive.

years before. More than ever, the farm took on the appearance of a Midwestern dairy. To complete the modernization, Anna and Charlie oversaw the construction of a bottling plant and ordered new milking and ice machines to keep up with an increasing market for ice cream.

After construction on the barn was complete, but before rounding up the cows for the winter, the Creamers hosted a first-class barn dance and hired Billie Root and his orchestra to provide the music. On August 22, 1938, with the last of the construction dirt swept up and the tables

BARN DANCE

The Event You Have Been Waiting For. Given on the completion of our new barn, and in appreciation of the years of splendid support by the people of Fairbanks.

The public is invited to come as our guests and dance from 9 until 12 to the music of Billy Root and his orchestra. The place is the second floor of our new, modern barn, and the time is 9 p.m. Tonight.

Overalls and ginghams—YES!
Dress Clothes—NO!

CREAMER'S DAIRY
The home of Quality Milk Products

Barn dance flyer (1938). Friends of Creamer's Field Photo Archives.

laid out with food and drink, Anna and Charlie greeted the arriving guests. Nearly everyone in Fairbanks turned out for the event, and cars were parked all along College Road. One thousand people joined in the dancing and took turns riding through the barn on the new manure cart. As things wound down, Creamer's ice cream was served. Then, with waves and calls of thanks, tired but happy townsfolk rode back to their cars on College Road in a wagon drawn by four stately Percherons.

Don was 16 when the first Louden barn was built. He helped haul lumber and ran back and forth to provide a saw here and a hammer there. A few weeks after the big barn dance, Don had his own party. One of the "ladies from the alcohol manufacturing business" fixed him up with four or five gallons of grain alcohol. Don mixed up 30 gallons of punch with plenty of ice. The young crowd played records on the old RCA and tried for radio reception by running a wire up and out of the loft. And, of course, they rode the manure train "after they got to feeling pretty good."

Further modernization occurred simultaneously for the Creamer and Bentley dairies. In November 1940, both dairies installed pasteurizing equipment to keep up with national health standards. On December 31, 1940, the Creamers ran a full-page ad in the local paper to inform the public of their new pasteurization process, stating that they had invested $20,000. In the advertisement, they provided an overview of the milking and bottling methods. Essentially, after milking the cows, Charlie and his crew poured the raw milk into a large cooling tank and then routed it to the pasteurizer, a heated vat that brought milk up to 145 degrees for a minimum of 30 minutes, effectively killing most bacteria while retaining the milk's natural flavor. After pasteurization, the milk again entered a cooling unit where it was chilled to 38 degrees prior to bottling. A bottling machine then filled the glass bottles, a capper capped them, and the bottles were placed in cases for delivery. A bottle washer cleaned the returning bottles with a pressure soak using a150-degree alkali solution followed by a chlorinated bath before the final rinse. The Creamers also invested in a machine to homogenize the milk used in making ice cream. This process broke up the liquid milk and cream into minute particles for a smoother, more consistent texture.

Birds During the Farming Years

Located approximately five miles north of the Tanana River and adjacent to sloughs that had once branched from the river, the Creamers' farm lay along the principal migration corridor taken by Lesser Sandhill Cranes and a vast number of ducks and geese on their passage to and from the Yukon-Kuskokwim Delta each spring and fall. Over the years, as the Creamers cleared trees and cultivated the soil, the farm became an important stopover for weary birds en route.

Each spring, in preparation for planting, Charlie and his crew shoveled up the manure that had accumulated near the barn all winter and spread it on the fields as fertilizer. Its dark color sped up snowmelt, and because it contained undigested grain, waterfowl were attracted to the fields as they migrated north from wintering grounds in the south.

Charlie enjoyed the birds, and he swept up spilled grain around the dairy and spread it for them when they began to arrive in the spring. The birds did not interfere with the crops because they left for their nesting grounds before spring planting. Spring duck hunting became illegal in 1918 due to declining bird populations, but many hunters disregarded the regulations. However, Charlie did not allow hunting on his land. He reasoned that the birds paired for life, and shooting any would result in fewer birds for the next generation.

In 1937, spring arrived late, and the ducks were two weeks behind schedule when they finally appeared on May 4. Thousands of ducks, many more than in previous years, descended on the fields and began to search for food. Apparently, snow had covered their normal feeding stops en route, and the birds were starving. Charlie took it upon himself to feed them, spreading peas and oats, which they eagerly consumed. The local papers reported that the dairy "looked more like a duck ranch than a cow farm." As warm weather melted the snow in the fields, the ducks, mostly Northern Pintails, gathered in the resulting melt ponds along with a number of Lesser Sandhill Cranes. The influx of birds continued for two weeks, and they became so tame that they waddled right into the barn among the cows to solicit handouts. By June 9, the birds had moved on, and Charlie planted his fields and turned his cows out to graze, running three weeks late himself due to the long winter.

Because of the level of human activity on Creamer's Field, the majority of birds typically made their spring and fall rest stops at the Experimental Farm west of town and out on the grain fields along Farmer's Loop Road. When many of these farms switched from grain crops to hay, more birds began to frequent the float ponds and open fields at the city and military airports. This posed flight risks, and in the mid-1940s, the Tanana Valley Sportsmen's Association began to purchase and spread grain for the birds at Creamer's Dairy and at the Experimental Farm. The grain drew the birds away from the airports, and their numbers increased greatly at both farms. The presence of so many birds drew townsfolk and school groups to the dairy. School children had long come to tour the dairy and watch the milking process, now they came to study the birds as well. The arrival of waterfowl at Creamer's Dairy came to be viewed as a harbinger of spring in Fairbanks.

Birds congregate on spring melt ponds. Photograph by Ken Whitten.

Cow Jumping over the Moon

Mallard

Chapter Six

Changes During and after World War II

In Europe, events culminating in the Second World War escalated daily as France and England joined in the fight against Germany. Alaska, remote and unprotected, appeared vulnerable, and in 1939 construction began on Ladd Field, just east of town (later renamed Fort Wainwright). As the war progressed, construction of airstrips and barracks went into overdrive, and work proceeded throughout the winter. By summer, 1,000 men worked to cover three shifts a day. The base opened for operations in September 1940.

On December 7, 1941, Japan bombed Pearl Harbor, Hawaii, and the United States found itself swept up in the Second World War. Construction of the Alaska-Canadian Military Highway began in April 1942 and was completed between Fairbanks and Dawson Creek, Canada, in a remarkable eight months. Built to provide access to airstrips and to facilitate the delivery of military equipment, the road was initially closed to civilian traffic. As the war escalated, men throughout the Interior honored the call to enlist and left Alaska to serve. Once again, as with the First World War, Fairbanks businesses faced a shortage of skilled farmhands and laborers, and the impact on the dairy was immediate. On December 18, 1941, Charlie wrote Governor Ernest Gruening to request some leniency in the draft for dairy workers:

> *Now another very serious situation has arrived; the Army is drafting all the young men. I am supplying Ladd Field and most of the city. We are running 90 head of stock, and we have a large investment, too large to run without help. I have had to take one of the trucks myself and I should be on the place to oversee things. It's so hard now at my age to work like this. I will be obliged to cut down the herd of cattle unless there is some way I can keep these men I have trained. I had to take my son out of college in March to take one of the delivery trucks. I hated to take him from his school, but I could not get anyone, so he had to take a truck. And he had worked every day and Sundays too, all summer.*

Despite his appeal to the governor, Charlie and Anna lost most of their skilled workers to the war. On October 1, 1942, the Creamers stopped making home deliveries because they lacked drivers to run the routes, but they kept up deliveries to local restaurants and grocery stores.

Initially, milk went from 25 cents a quart to 45 cents a quart during the war years. The Creamers still delivered milk in glass bottles, but these became increasingly difficult to resupply. Charlie established military contracts with Ladd Field, and instead of running three trucks around town on home-delivery routes, he made one large delivery to the base, where he sold milk, ice cream, cottage cheese, and buttermilk. The base, in turn, provided a source of part-time laborers with soldiers pitching in during their off-duty hours.

By June 1943, both the Creamer and Bentley dairies suspended all bottled milk delivery due to labor shortages and price fixing by the Office of Price Administration. The high cost of maintaining operations could not be offset by the fixed price of 20 cents a quart set for milk and 69 cents a pound for butter. Moreover, by June, Charlie was so shorthanded that he had not yet planted his fields, putting him three weeks behind the growing season. To cope, the Creamers dedicated all production to their military contract and hoped to avoid butchering their milk cows. Charlie contracted with the military to reconstitute powdered milk the military supplied by adding sweet cream, which increased the milk fat to between three and three-and-one-half percent.

Don worked long hours at the dairy with Charlie and made most of the deliveries to the base. But he found time to do a little courting and soon found a young woman with whom to share his life. In November 1943, Don Creamer and Connie Allyn were wed. Don was 21 and Connie was just 18. Connie soon became pregnant with their first child, but in 1944, before the birth of Jeannie Creamer, Don was drafted.

Don wondered if someone on the draft board had it out for him. Eddie Clausen, manager of the NC Company, became greatly upset with the Creamers after they ceased store deliveries. According to Don, Eddie figured, "If you're going to give the army all your milk, your kid can go too." Farm workers could get draft exemptions, but somehow,

Don's did not come through. He served 23 weeks at Fort Richardson in Anchorage, and then the army assigned him to Shemya Air Force Base on Alaska's Aleutian chain.

While Don was in the service, Charlie and Anna cut back on the herd, paring down to 40 milk cows from the 50 they had previously maintained to reduce milk production. On June 4, 1945, Charlie's mother, Minnie, died from a stroke. C.N. Creamer died just four months later, on October 10. On the same day that C.N. died, an article in the *Fairbanks Daily News-Miner* stated that the Creamers would accept offers for the purchase of their herd, stating that the dairy would likely close due to the difficulty in securing sufficient staff. The Chamber of Commerce, looking to avoid a milk crisis during the winter, appealed to the Director of Selective Services to release Don Creamer from military service so that he could return to the farm.

Don applied for and was assigned to Ladd Air Force Base, and finally, in 1946, he was discharged and returned to the farm. Once he returned, delivery routes resumed and the Creamers began to increase their herd size again. The population of Fairbanks expanded as enlisted service members returned home, and the presence of the military base just outside the city provided the dairy with a steady source of business and revenue.

Creamer's Dairy Production Increases

In 1947, after a four-year wartime delay for material delivery, the Creamers oversaw the construction of a second Louden barn. It had the same dimensions but lacked the extra ten feet of height that gave the first barn such a distinctive stature. This barn held an additional 50 cows and hay to feed them through the winter. In 1949, Charlie and Anna extended

Don a one-third partnership in the dairy. With the closure of the Bentley Dairy in 1950, the Creamers' business flourished.

The herd grew to 80 milk cows, along with 30 to 40 dry heifers kept as reserve stock. The dairy sold 250 to 300 gallons of Grade A milk and up to 600 gallons of ice cream daily, along with sherbet, cottage cheese, whipping cream, buttermilk, chocolate milk, and an orange-flavored drink.

The full-time workforce increased from 12 to 18 people between 1950 and 1960. Workers were provided with housing, consisting of small cabins for married men and a bunkhouse for single men. Anna continued to provide meals for the single men, and over the years, she hired women to assist in the kitchen.

Creamer family and crew with new 1951 International Harvester Van. Back row: Don, Charlie, and Anna Creamer, William Oskam, Sr., William Hurtz, Frank Cloud, Noeta Cloud, and William Oskam, Jr. Kneeling: Albin Rief, unknown, Wes Wright (circa 1951). Creamer Family Collection, Friends of Creamer's Field Photo Archives.

Growing Up as Farm Kids

Work on the farm never ceased, but Anna and Charlie always made time for their grandchildren. Don and Connie had six children over a span of sixteen years—Jeannie, Charles, Donald, Clifford, Roxanne, and Jeffery. Don and his family lived on the farm in a house to the east of the main house, but the farmhouse remained the central hub of activity. Over the years, the Creamers built several small houses for workers and their families to live in, and a community took shape on the farm.

Jeannie's earliest memories include following her Grandpa Charlie everywhere as he went about the business of running the farm. He had a wonderful way with animals, always patient and soft-spoken. And he never seemed to mind having Jeannie, his little shadow, close beside him as he worked.

The farm was an ideal place for rambunctious children. The pond behind the barns (now called the seasonal pond) filled with snowmelt and became a swimming hole each summer. On clear summer nights, as the sun hung low over Ester Dome, an open field invited baseball games. The Tanana Valley State Fair took place each summer just west of the dairy, and the children slipped under the fence to save the fifty-cent entry fee. Over the Fourth of July, there were firecrackers. (The Roman candles were saved for wintertime, when it was dark enough to see them.) In the winter, the haylofts provided a warm place to play, and by flooding one of the corrals, the children formed an ice skating rink right there on the farm.

The farm had an assortment of animals in addition to the cows. Grandma Anna kept chickens and pigs while the barns were home to numerous cats and kittens, and the family always had a dog to pal along on the day's adventures. The farm and surrounding woodlands attracted wild animals, too, primarily moose, fox, and the occasional black bear or coyote. One year, before the children were born, a small herd of caribou came bounding over the fence along College Road. When Don went out to tend to the cows, there were caribou among them. Sometimes, Alaska Fish and Game employees brought out orphaned animals in need of fostering. Once, they brought a moose calf that quickly bonded with the children and followed them everywhere.*

Like many young girls, Jeannie developed a love of horses. But there were no riding horses at the farm, so she asked her father for one. Don denied her repeated requests until Grandma Anna took up the cause. Anna remembered her days of riding as a girl and argued that Jeannie would benefit from working with a horse. Don reconsidered and bought a horse for Jeannie at the town rodeo. The horse, a bay gelding named Blaze, did not like men. Charlie attempted to train him but finally gave up in frustration. Jeannie took up the challenge, and the horse turned out to be gentle around children. Jeannie spent many summer days riding him around the farm and the surrounding countryside. Don later bought an American saddlebred gelding from Dr. John Weston in town. This horse appeared to limp badly, but in truth, he was just a good actor. Jeannie rode him even though he had the habit of kicking up his back legs and pitching off his riders. He was fast, and Jeannie delighted in outracing her horseback-riding friends. Later that summer, the family paired the

* See Appendix B: Mammals of Creamer's Field Migratory Waterfowl Refuge.

horse with a former jockey who worked at the dairy, and together they won a race at the Tanana Valley Fair.

Several times throughout the year, the Creamers' extended family got together. Charlie's sisters came with their families, and the house spilled over with cousins. Connie played piano, Bill Stroecker played trumpet, and everyone sang along. Connie's parents lived in town, too. Grandpa Allyn had a good singing voice, and some people said he only attended church because he liked to sing.

One of Jeannie's favorite memories was of movie night. Several times a month, Don or Charlie rented a movie from the Co-Op, usually a cartoon or Western, and Anna cooked up a big batch of popcorn. Everyone came to watch, farm workers and families alike. They crowded into the family room in Don's house and hand-cranked ice cream, with each kid taking a turn until their arm gave out. It was one of many ways the Creamers built a family and a community on the farm.

Charlie Takes Up Potato Farming

Despite the surge in milk consumption after World War II, profits at the dairy were never dependable. Seeking to diversify, Charlie bid on and won a contract to supply the military with potatoes. He selected a site off Farmer's Loop Road (land that would later become the Jeff Studdert Race Grounds) and planted 50 acres of potatoes.

He tried Arctic seedling potatoes, white rose potatoes, and a variety of red potatoes. Potatoes grew well in Alaska and were free of the blights that affected potato crops in the rest of the United States. Charlie's crop flourished, and in early September, when fall breezes shook the golden leaves from the birch trees, Charlie prepared for the harvest. He hired 150 potato pickers and, of course, the grandkids came too. Charlie rounded up everyone willing to work—folks coming in from the mines, military boys with farming backgrounds, and anyone with a good back.

Charlie dug the potatoes with a mechanical potato digger, turning the fields over first thing in the morning and allowing them to dry a little. Then, by nine or ten o'clock, everyone piled into the flatbed trucks and headed out with gunnysacks and lunch baskets to make a day of it.

They freed the potatoes from the soil and loaded them into the gunnysacks, making their way steadily down the rows. In the late afternoon, as daylight waned, Charlie forked over a few final rows. With their backs aching from bending over, the potato pickers found those potatoes more by feel than by sight. Then, brushing the dirt from their farm clothes, they all climbed back into the trucks and made the trip home. Over the next few days, the potatoes were washed and sorted in the farmhouse root cellar. Any damaged potatoes were culled and fed to the cows, who ate them with pleasure. Charlie met his contract with the military and had potatoes left over to sell in the grocery stores. He stayed in the potato business for about 20 years but never found it to be as lucrative as he had hoped.

Transportation Advances and Competition

While the Creamers realized strong sales and growth during the 1950s, they began to face competition from dairies in the Lower 48. As early as 1936, a word-of-mouth campaign from stateside dairies conveyed the notion that milk from Alaska lacked vitamin D because of the long winter months. The Creamers attempted to counter this rumor by running radio and newspaper advertisements to correct the misinformation and point out the benefits of buying fresh local milk.

When the military lifted travel restrictions on the Alaska-Canadian Highway in 1948, farmers and dairymen from the Lower 48 states quickly expanded their marketing to Fairbanks. In June 1951, the Fairbanks International Airport opened at its new location southwest of town, offering longer runways and better operations. Because of their relatively low operating costs and shipping subsidies, large stateside dairies like Carnation and Arden flew milk to Fairbanks and sold it at prices that undercut Creamer's Dairy prices. The Creamers dropped their prices to remain competitive, and their profits fell to just a one or two percent return on their investment. When dairies across the country went to paper cartons, Creamer's Dairy began using paper cartons, too, although they stayed with glass

Charlie Creamer with new ice cream making equipment (circa 1950). Nona Johnson Collection, Friends of Creamer's Field Photo Archives.

bottles for home delivery. Despite these changes, the Outside dairies soon dominated the market on Fairbanks grocery store shelves.

Closer to home, in the spring of 1954, the Matanuska Valley Cooperative Association in Palmer, Alaska, bought the Fairbanks Laundry building at 124 Second Avenue and established a milk processing plant for small local farmers, directly competing with Creamer's Dairy. When Charlie first got wind of the Association's plans to locate a branch in Fairbanks, he appealed to the Fairbanks City Council not to proceed with a proposed tax incentive for the Association. He estimated his investment in the dairy to be $500,000 with 120 head of stock and $40,000 in improvements made during the last year. Nonetheless, the new dairy plant opened on June 18, 1954, and was deemed the most modern in Alaska. Competition from the Matanuska Valley Cooperative Association processing plant continued until 1962 when they closed the Fairbanks operation due to an insufficient supply of local milk.

Dairy Regulations Tighten with Statehood

While competition from local and Outside milk processors resulted in a significant decrease in store sales, Creamer's Dairy still had military contracts, home-delivery routes, and most of the business from local restaurants. The Creamers adjusted by using surplus milk to increase their ice cream production even though ice cream did not provide as much profit. On April 9, 1959, Charlie and Anna, along with Don and Connie, assumed a new $120,000 mortgage on the dairy through refinancing. They invested in new bottle-washing equipment and an automatic capper to better meet their contract with the military, knowing it would take four or five years to make good on the investment.

To compound their difficulties, Creamer's Dairy came under increasing pressure from sanitation inspectors to comply with national health standards. Nationwide, mechanization and more stringent sanitation regulations greatly increased the capital needed to maintain a state-certified dairy. The trend stateside was for consolidation of dairies, with fewer dairies producing more milk. Once Alaska became a state in January 1959, its dairies came under strict federal sanitation requirements.

Twenty years before, Charlie had been progressive with his silos and protein-rich forage, which resulted in increased milk yields. The barn, once state-of-the-art, now needed an expensive upgrade. Charlie's workers had always milked the cows in their stalls, tying up their tails to prevent them from contaminating the milk. But the cows frequently lay down in their stalls and there was no easy way to keep them clean, despite hosing the stalls daily. Workers washed the cows' flanks with chlorine, but bacteria counts in the milk often exceeded federal limits. To comply with the new standards, the dairy needed to build a loafing shed for washing cows daily and a milking parlor for milking separate from any other activity. Milk had to be piped in stainless steel tubing to the milk house, where it would be cooled immediately, resulting in less handling and reduced contamination.

State inspectors walked through the dairy, clipboards in hand, and pointed out their concerns. The buildings had problems with moisture, even with the fans going, and drying by heating the cavernous barns was prohibitively expensive. Sewage runoff created another problem. The Creamers had always hosed out the barns and let the

Aerial view of Creamer's Dairy (May 20, 1960). Friends of Creamer's Field Photo Archives.

rinse water run into the slough just west of the barns. But the slough was frozen solid for seven months of the year. Charlie and Anna needed to build a sewer system. Then coliform counts at the dairy exceeded milk quality standards one too many times, and the story made the local papers. Anna and Charlie could not see any way to afford further modernization, and the strain began to wear them down. Always known for his gentleness, Charlie got so angry with one inspector that he took the man roughly by the shoulder and escorted him from the building. Because of sanitation concerns, the military did not renew their annual contract. The loss dealt a terrible blow to the dairy, which was overextended with debt.

Don, Connie, Charlie, and Anna struggled to find a solution to their troubles while sitting around the table in the farmhouse kitchen, and out of worry and frustration, their conversations often deteriorated into arguments. Connie kept the books by then and knew how bleak their finances were. Don suggested improvements, but Charlie and Anna did not want to upgrade if it meant more debt. Don grew discouraged and wanted to leave the dairy business, but Charlie and Anna talked him into staying time and again.

The Writing on the Wall

With their best years behind them, Charlie and Anna were losing ground. The buildup of the military in Alaska provided good-paying jobs that did not necessitate working 70 or 80 hours a week, so securing and retaining a good crew required higher pay for fewer hours. Farms outside of Alaska reduced labor costs through increased mechanization. In Alaska, farmers faced excessive transportation costs for equipment, a limited distribution range for the crops they raised, and the increased availability of goods freighted up from the Lower 48. Not surprisingly, farming settlements in Alaska never expanded throughout the agriculturally viable regions as they did in the Lower 48 and Canada.

State sanitation requirements, while sound in principle, put the burden of implementation on Alaskan dairies at a time when Outside competition dramatically reduced profits. Even in dairies outside of Alaska, compliance with newer health standards took time. A 1980 survey of New York State dairies found that 80 percent of dairies still lacked modern milking parlors and one-third were still using the mobile milking machine that had been introduced just after the turn of the century; these dairies transported milk to cooling vats using buckets rather than using stainless steel tubing. Anna and Charlie Creamer were both in their seventies when they were confronted by the insurmountable obstacles imposed by competition, tighter sanitation regulations, and state taxes. The realization that the dairy was sadly outdated and financially overextended must have been overwhelming.

Faced with a $175,000 mortgage and dwindling sales, they knew they needed to sell. Connie and Don separated that same year. Then, on October 14, 1965 Anna Creamer died. She was 80 years old. Charlie was 76 and had been in the dairy business for 38 years, working seven days a week the entire time.

Anna and Charlie Creamer (circa 1957). Friends of Creamer's Field Photo Archives.

Early in 1966, the First National Bank of Fairbanks, with William "Bill" Stroecker as president, foreclosed but gave the Creamers time to try to sell the land. Charlie and Don had 108 cows when they turned them out of the barns that summer and dried them up. Their milking days were over. In the fall, Charlie and Don slaughtered the animals and sold the meat. They piled the beef they could not sell out back for the foxes, as they could not afford refrigeration. Years later, the bones remained as a grim reminder of all that once was.

Boreal and Black-Capped Chickadee

Canada Geese

Chapter Seven

From Farm to Wildlife Management Area

By the late 1960s, the Creamer's farm and the city were rubbing shoulders as new houses, schools, and businesses crowded up against the eastern and southern borders of the verdant farmland. Such a parcel of land, so close to the city's core, offered highly desirable building sites with well-drained soils, a flat grade, and proximity to power, water, and major roadways.

Fortunately, another option came into play. This small farm, developed over 65 years through the toil and determination of two families, now inspired a community. The people of Fairbanks felt a connection to the place. They set their spring clocks by the arrival of the first geese on the fields each April. In the winter, area mushers raced dog teams across the snowy fields and into the woodlands beyond.

The dairy inspired nostalgia because it had grown up with and alongside the city. The farm offered a sense of place at the heart of a community experiencing rapid change, and it did that through its history, its ties to the community, and the pastoral setting it preserved. As the dairy declined, a new purpose for the land took shape.

Fairbanks Citizens Organize to Save the Farmland

In October 1966, Charlie and Don contacted area realtors to inform them of the availability of the farm. In the *Fairbanks Daily News-Miner,* Charlie stated that taxes "are just too high to keep going" and that he hoped to avoid subdividing the land. Fairbanks Realty listed the farm and soon had a buyer for 100 acres on the southeast corner. The construction of Joy Elementary School and Wedgewood Manor Apartments soon followed on that parcel. Additional acreage along Farmer's Loop Road was also sold. Soon, just 259 acres remained.

As fate would have it, a few years before the dairy went up for sale, a group of locals attending a monthly Alaska Conservation Society (ACS) meeting had considered purchasing the dairy. On a spring day, Celia Hunter, Ginny Wood, Bob Weeden, Leslie Viereck, Dan Swift, and ACS president Jane Williams met over brown bag lunches in a room at the University of Alaska. Small talk circulated about the weather and the arrival of birds at Creamer's Dairy. Someone voiced a thought: Wouldn't it be wonderful if they could purchase the dairy someday so that school children and area residents could continue to enjoy the open space and the birds?

When the dairy became available for purchase, ACS members quickly sought to raise public interest in purchasing the land for use as an educational and recreational site. Elbert Rice, head of the University of

Alaska Civil Engineering Department and an ACS member, organized a public meeting on May 1, 1967, to discuss the purchase of the property. Twenty-five people turned out for the meeting, including Fairbanks North Star Borough Planning Director Donn Hopkins and Borough Assembly Chairman Harold Gillam. Hopkins and Gillam recognized the land's potential and, upon their recommendation, the Borough Assembly authorized $2,500 in Borough funds to study the potential for developing recreational and educational facilities on the property. The National Audubon Society's Nature Center Division would conduct the study. However, the Borough did not have the budget to purchase recreational land, and the city could not fund the purchase because the dairy lay outside the Fairbanks city limits. It would be up to the State of Alaska to appropriate the purchase price for the property.

The Alaska Department of Fish and Game requested that the United States Fish and Wildlife Service conduct an analysis of the site to determine if the land met the Federal Aid for Wildlife Restoration Program's requirements. An expert from the Portland Regional Office came to Fairbanks two weeks later, on May 15, 1967, to make the determination. The Bureau's findings concluded that the land was an established stopover for waterfowl during their spring and fall migrations and qualified for federal funding under the Pittman-Robertson Act, P.L. 75-415. This fund was financed by a national tax on the sale of guns and ammunition intended for the preservation or improvement of land used by wildlife for feeding, resting, or breeding. The fund would provide 75 percent of the purchase price, provided the State of Alaska could provide the remaining 25 percent.

That same month, on May 2, Alaska Governor Walter J. Hickel toured the farm while on a visit to Fairbanks for the Alaska 67 Exposition, a celebration of the centennial of the Alaska Purchase at the newly completed Alaskaland, a historical site featuring many of Fairbanks' oldest buildings (now Pioneer Park). He was aware of the pending legislation to purchase the farmland for a wildlife management area, and after visiting the farm, he returned to Juneau in support of the purchase.

The Flood of 1967

The August rains of 1967 caused a brief setback in the efforts to purchase the farm. August in Interior Alaska is predictably rainy, but that year, with the ground already saturated from a wetter-than-normal June and July, heavy rains forced the Chena River over its banks on August 14. The water crept higher, lapping over curbs and driveways and inundating basements. The swirling floodwaters continued to rise throughout the day and into the night, and some 15,000 people headed to higher ground at the university, Eielson Air Force Base, and Lathrop High School.

The city's hospital flooded, and all the patients had to be moved to Bassett Army Hospital on Fort Wainwright. Homes and businesses stood in water four feet deep or more, and power was out all over town for up to a week. Parked cars were submerged, and the roads became channels for canoes and motorboats with road signs jutting up from the surging waters. Creamer's Dairy did not escape the flood, and the cold brown water filled the farmhouse basement and flowed over the cork floors in the barns. Governor Hickel declared Fairbanks a disaster area. The water receded within a week, but months of work lay ahead as Fairbanks shoveled mud and sorted through debris. Property damages reached $85 million, making it the worst disaster in the city's history.

Money Is Raised to Secure the Land

Two months after the flood, the State had not yet signed an agreement with the Creamers to purchase the dairy, and private developers jotted down numbers with an eye toward subdividing the farm into residential lots. The Alaska Conservation Society knew the Creamers might have a lucrative offer any day and realized they had to act quickly. ACS hoped a fund drive would raise enough money for a down payment on the land until the State could authorize funding for the full purchase price. But could the people of Fairbanks, still recovering from the devastation of the August flood, raise the money needed?

On November 21, ACS members approached Charlie and Don, asking them (in Don's words), "Do you want to sell, or do you want a park?"

Charlie hated to see the wildlife and birds displaced and felt strongly that the land should remain as open fields. Don and Charlie signed an agreement with ACS stating that they would hold off on any offers to buy the farm until December 1. That gave ACS just ten days to raise $5,000 in earnest money toward the purchase price of the farm.

ACS members, most notably ADF&G biologist Bob Weeden, scrambled to get the word out, approaching area businesses, schools, and outdoor user groups. Fairbanks responded with a passion that surprised everyone, and funds began to come in even before an account was set up to receive them. The Campfire Girls at University Park Elementary School baked cakes with mixes donated from local stores and raised $82 at their bake sale. Local dog musher and writer Mary Shields attended school fundraising events with a Great Horned Owl riding on her shoulder to draw attention to the needs of wildlife in the area. Students from Nordale Elementary donated money they had set aside for a Christmas gift exchange. Eielson High School held a dance, and the $350 they raised in admission fees went to the fund. Dog mushers, bird watchers, and other outdoor enthusiasts who had long frequented the fields during different times of year responded with support as well. The fund drive was truly a grassroots effort, spearheaded in large part by the city's children. But by December 1, only $2,000 of the $5,000 needed had been raised. ACS went to the Creamers and asked for an extension. The Creamers consented and extended the agreement until December 8.

The money continued to trickle in, and at 3:00 p.m. on December 7, Denali Park Elementary made a $124 contribution to cap the $5,000 goal. Still donations kept coming, with a total of $6,800 raised by over 200 individuals, businesses, and schools. The Golden Nugget Skydivers provided an exhibition jump marking the end of the drive.

Charlie and Don Creamer signed the option agreement with ACS on December 15, 1967. They agreed to sell 259 acres at a price of $268,000. This included all the dairy land except for the farm buildings and the 12 acres surrounding them. Don and Charlie wanted between $100,000 and $200,000 for the dairy buildings and adjacent land, though the State had assessed their value at only $28,700, so the buildings were not included in the sale. ACS held the option on the 259 acres while the State of Alaska prepared to appropriate money for the actual purchase. The option agreement was to be binding until April 15, 1968.

In early 1968, ACS initiated a property assessment through Meyers Real Estate. This assessment arrived at a value of between $210,000 and $271,000 without the farm buildings and equipment. The low price reflected the option of selling the land as a whole to a sub-developer while the high price factored in selling it as individual lots with roads and utilities provided. ACS then approached Don and Charlie with a modified contract, and the Creamers agreed to adjust the purchase price to $225,000.

State and Federal Revenues Finalize the Sale

The land purchasc proceeded smoothly once the price was agreed upon. State Senators John Butrovich and Paul Haggland, both of Fairbanks, introduced Senate Bill 368 on February 17, 1968, requesting that $56,250 from the Legislative General Fund be appropriated to ADF&G for the State's agreed-upon 25 percent of the purchase price. The bill passed in the State Senate and House, and Governor Hickel signed it into law on April 17, 1968. The State monies came from a fund financed by the sale of hunting licenses for the purpose of enhancing the access to and quality of wildlife resources. ADF&G then applied for and received $168,750 from the Pittman-Robertson Funds.

On May 29, 1968, the 259 acres on College Road became the property of the people of Alaska, and ADF&G assumed management of the new Fairbanks Wildlife Management Area (FWMA). In June of the same year, ADF&G applied for the transfer of 1,520 acres of adjacent State land to be included in the Wildlife Management Area. The transfer came through in 1970, and its addition to the FWMA brought the management area to nearly 1,800 acres.

The members of ACS were ecstatic. The timing could not have been more critical as oil was discovered in Prudhoe Bay in the spring of 1968, and land prices immediately began to climb. ACS member Celia Hunter later stated that with the "subsequent, frantic development that went on in Fairbanks, we would not have had a prayer of holding that choice piece of real estate along College Road in a nature preserve. We got that area at probably the last moment that it was possible to get a large chunk of land as a green belt along College Road."

Uses of the Land as a Wildlife Management Area

When the State assumed ownership of the wildlife management area, Charlie and Don still owned and inhabited the 12 acres that included the farmhouse and the surrounding buildings. The only road into the newly acquired management area was essentially their driveway. In 1969, ADF&G and the Alaska Department of Natural Resources, working under an interagency land management agreement, installed a parking area just off College Road where people could park to view the ducks and geese on the fields.

Because the fields had lain fallow during 1967, the Tanana Valley Sportsmen's Association, ACS, and the Fairbanks Bird Club donated grain to spread in the fields for the incoming birds during the spring of 1968. Thereafter, the Borealis Kiwanis Club and North Pole High School Future Farmers of America assumed the responsibility of providing grain.

Area volunteers began organizing community events at Creamer's Field soon after the land came under State ownership. As early as 1967, naturalists Mary Shields and

Canada geese in repose amid feeding Sandhill Cranes. Friends of Creamer's Field Photo Archives.

Gail Mayo organized walks for local school children. Initially called Spring Migration Bird Watch, Mary and Gail offered the event to children in kindergarten through second grade. Over time, they also developed activities for older children, emphasizing bird identification and behavior. The annual event became the Fifth Grade Bird Watch. Over the ensuing years, thousands of students have lined the edge of the fields to learn about the behavior and needs of migrating waterfowl. As of 2025, this program is still held annually.

To better educate the public on the many birds frequenting the front fields, local artists Bill Berry and George West made signs in the late 1960s for the south edge of the fields. Then, on April 21, 1969, Charlie presided as judge of the first annual Goose Classic, which the KFAR radio station sponsored. The event provided a cash prize to the person who most closely guessed when the first goose would land at Creamer's Field each spring. This became an annual event, continuing until the late 1990s.

Meanwhile, Don and Charlie Creamer, having been paid in full by the State for the land, returned the $6,800 earnest money they had received from ACS. After some deliberation, ACS decided not to attempt to return the money to the different community contributors. Instead, they set it aside for future educational purposes. ACS put the money into a separate savings account where it drew interest, and over time they forgot about it.

The next project to take place on the fields left no doubt about the role of ADF&G in the management area. The State Court Building on Barnette Street housed ADF&G staff, but space became increasingly limited as new staff joined the Department. The management area provided an attractive site for a new regional office building. Controversy arose around concerns that the 11,700 square foot building would destroy the pastoral value of the farmlands and disturb migratory waterfowl. ADF&G countered this argument by stating that its presence in the management area would thwart some of the vandalism and harassment of wildlife that occurred. ADF&G built a $750,000 office building directly south of the farm buildings with easy access to College Road, completing the project in 1972.

What Became of the Creamers?

While ADF&G and various community groups contemplated how best to utilize the newly acquired management area, Charlie and Don worked about their 12 remaining acres to clean up and conclude 40 years of living there. They sold off the farming equipment at an auction and continued to seek a buyer for the buildings and the remaining land. On May 28, 1968, Charlie set out to tidy up around the buildings by burning the weeds and overgrown grass. The blaze got out of hand, and before Charlie could suppress the flames, Don's house caught fire. Don was asleep inside. He awoke in time to snatch up a few belongings before running from the burning building. The fire department was called, and eight fire trucks eventually responded to the blaze. At first, the wind blew to the east, but then it shifted west, raising concern that the barns would ignite. The fire was finally extinguished, but Don's home was reduced to a smoldering shell. Consequently, Don moved into the old farmhouse with Charlie.

Don found work driving a school bus during the winter. In the summer, he drove a tour bus in Denali National Park. Jeannie Creamer returned to Fairbanks after several years away at college to find that much had changed. But the birds and wildlife had been a wonderful part of growing up on the farm, and she was glad to see the land remain open for them.

In 1970 a land investment company run by Wally Burnett, Nick McWelsh, and Cliff Burglin bought the farmhouse. They used it primarily for storage, and the buildings, already showing their age, fell into disrepair. In May of 1973, a city tax inspector visited the property to assess its tax value and, according to his note, talked with Wally Burnett. He wrote that the buildings "reflect much damage and disrepair." Wally explained that the investment company only insured the bunkhouse and the small foreman's house, as those were both wired for electricity and in working order. They rented out the bunkhouse to the Bureau of Land Management for summer quarters for firefighters. The inspector stated in his notes that "Mr. Burnett said that they plan to tear down Building 3 sometime this year." Building 3, according to a small stack of photos taped into the tax files, was none other than the farmhouse.

For reasons unknown, the investment company did not tear down the farmhouse. It continued to stand, all but abandoned, with its once-white exterior fading to gray as the paint flaked away. Then, in 1977, despite the buildings' degraded condition, the National Park Service placed the farmhouse and barns on the National Register of Historic Places. This served to underscore their significance to the community and gave them a measure of protection.

Charlie moved to the Fairbanks Pioneer Home in 1973. He knew many of the residents living there and shared stories and memories with everyone who asked. His warm laugh and sense of humor never left him. He was 85 years old when he died on December 14, 1974. Don lived out the remaining years of his life in Fairbanks. He died from a stroke on August 19, 2003.

Creamer's farmhouse (circa 1985). John Wright Collection, Alaska Department of Fish and Game, Fairbanks Regional Office.

Chapter Eight

Managing a Migratory Waterfowl Refuge

Fairbanks changed rapidly during the 1970s due in large part to the construction of the TransAlaska Pipeline System and the jobs it created. The influx of pipeline workers and associated industries drove up land prices throughout the Interior, with property near the Fairbanks city center fetching premium prices. Amid a rapid transformation from woodlands to suburbs, the wildlife management area's open fields provided an opportunity for wildlife viewing and recreation.

Area residents frequented the trails throughout the year but found access during the summer months greatly restricted due to the marshy conditions on the northern half of the management area. In 1974, the Tanana-Yukon chapter of ACS applied for a grant from the American Revolution Bicentennial Commission to fund a boardwalk trail. In October 1975, it received the grant with the stipulation that the Tanana-Yukon chapter would provide matching funds. At about this same time, area manager Jerry McGowan skimmed an announcement in the *Fairbanks Daily News-Miner* notifying banking customers of inactive accounts. There, well down the page, was the account that had been established with the nearly $7,000 in earnest money that the Creamers had returned. This money provided the matching funds needed to construct a boardwalk through the forest. The State drew up plans for a two-mile-long interpretive trail (now known as the Boreal Forest Trail) based largely on an ecological survey conducted by University of Alaska graduate student Michael Andrew Spindler. Construction took place over the next two summers, with Gail Mayo as project leader. The Youth Conservation Corps provided the workforce and the grant covered the cost of materials. Gail kept the job moving along and supplied lemonade and cookies on hot afternoons to keep the young workers motivated.

In 1979, the management area became part of the Alaska State Game Refuge System and assumed the new title of Creamer's Field Migratory Waterfowl Refuge. In 1982, the Alaska legislature appropriated $2.5 million to purchase the farm buildings and the 12 acres surrounding them, and this, too, became part of the refuge system. Just 15 years earlier, the State could have purchased the property directly from the Creamers for a fraction of that amount.

Management of the historic Creamer's Dairy buildings fell to the Alaska Department of Fish and Game, and painting the well-weathered structures was one of the first projects that was completed after their purchase. In 1987, ADF&G decided that the Creamers' farmhouse should be remodeled to serve as a refuge headquarters, visitor center,

Remodeled farmhouse and barns. Photograph by Pamela Bergmann.

and office space for the nongame program. State Capital Improvement Project (CIP) funds not spent on painting could be used for the renovation. About $30,000 remained of the $150,000 Creamers' building CIP fund, and another $20,000 remained in a CIP fund administered by the State Division of Parks and Recreation. To conserve funds,

Camp Habitat in full swing (2025). Friends of Creamer's Field Photo Archives.

volunteers, Borealis Kiwanis Club, Key Club, and ADF&G staff took on the challenge of tearing out the old sheetrock, cabinets, wiring, plumbing, and chimney. Two laborers were later hired to complete the job. In 1989, ADF&G and the Alaska Craftsman Home Program signed a cooperative agreement for the farmhouse renovation. The project would demonstrate the use of energy conservation building practices in a retrofit project. Terry Duszynski guided the project, and under his leadership, most of the labor was donated by local contractors and much of the material was sold at cost. The farmhouse renovation was completed in 1991, and on April 29, 1995, (after completion of interpretive displays and furnishings), Don Creamer cut the ribbon to officially open the Farmhouse Visitor Center.

Volunteer Activities on the Refuge

As the farmhouse neared completion, Arctic Audubon Society and ADF&G began to discuss using the farmhouse as a nature education center. In 1990, ADF&G hired Jim Chumbley as a refuge assistant. He organized a group of about thirty people (which later became the Friends of Creamer's Field) who brainstormed and "dreamed big," according to Susan Grace Stoltz, who attended that first meeting in the farmhouse. They saw a need to offer free educational programs to the public, thus making the refuge an integral part of the Fairbanks community.

Other developments unfolded on the refuge as well. In 1991, Susan Grace organized the first Camp Habitat, a summer day camp to be held on the refuge. All these years later, Camp Habitat continues to offer innovative environmental education to area children through hands-on experience, including hikes, games, and special projects.

Also in 1991, ADF&G hired Kris Hartnett (later Kris Nemeth) to oversee funding for and development of the nature center. Kris also established a spring training program for volunteers in preparation for a series of summer walks to be offered to area and out-of-town visitors. The walks began in 1992.

Kris raised grant money and consulted with experts to design an interpretive and educational facility within the newly remodeled farmhouse. Arctic Audubon Society contributed its $30,000 legislative grant to be used for a nature center at Creamer's Field. An agreement between the United States Fish and Wildlife Service, the Alaska Department of Fish and Game, Ducks Unlimited, North Star Flying Lions, Arctic Audubon Society, and Friends of Creamer's Field paved the way for a cooperative effort to develop interpretive exhibits in the Farmhouse Visitor Center and construct new nature trails with interpretive signs. Displays of the refuge's natural and cultural history now fill the front rooms, once the Creamers' dining and living rooms. In what was Anna's kitchen and office, shelves brim with field guides and books on natural history, plus an assortment of bird nests and other hands-on artifacts.

After Kris Nemeth left in 1996, Mark D. Ross was hired as a biologist in charge of education and interpretive programs. His skills as an illustrator and his keen observations of nature served him well as he developed and delivered popular school and public programs. Mark retired in 2025 and continues to volunteer with Friends of Creamer's Field.

In 1992, ADF&G invited a young biologist, Tom Pogson, to develop a migratory songbird banding station on the refuge. As executive director, Tom trained a staff of highly motivated area volunteers and college interns, and his fledgling organization, the Alaska Bird Observatory (ABO), set up a series of nets on the refuge. Throughout the spring and again in the fall (beginning in late April and concluding in early October), a crew of yawning, blurry-eyed ABO bird handlers would gather at what substitutes for dawn during Alaska's shoulder seasons. At 6:00 each morning (or a little later in the fall as daylight wanes), they opened mist nets, slogging through wetlands and waving away the infernal mosquitoes. For their efforts, they were rewarded with tiny songbirds that fluttered like colorful leaves in the nets. These birds were identified, measured, and fitted with a numbered leg band before being released. The data gathered contributed to a growing volume of knowledge about the physiological conditions and productivity by comparing the ratios of adults to offspring. Over the years, an overall decline in migratory songbird

Male Wilson's Warbler at the Alaska Songbird Institute field station. Alaska Songbird Institute Archives.

populations in Alaska's Interior has become apparent, as is true throughout the lower 48 states.

Operations moved to the second floor of the farmhouse as ABO staff increased, and Nancy DeWitt stepped in as executive director when Tom resigned in the summer of 1997. ABO shared the farmhouse with Friends of Creamer's Field volunteer staff until March 2002. In 2001–2002, Fountainhead Development, Inc. designed and constructed a spacious new office, complete with classroom space, to meet ABO's growing needs. Located just outside the eastern boundary of the refuge at Wedgewood Resort, the new location was convenient to visitors, and ABO staff had easy access to the refuge.

When the Alaska Bird Observatory closed in December 2012, a new organization was created, the Alaska Songbird Institute (ASI). Founded in January 2013, its initial work was to sustain and develop two community-based avian research projects at Creamer's Field Migratory Waterfowl Refuge—the Creamer's Field Migration Station and the Tree Swallow Ecology Project. ASI is ongoing and has expanded over the years, combining community science and robust research, outreached through social media and online articles.*

Meanwhile, the farmhouse has become the gathering place for year-round events organized by Friends of Creamer's Field. Each April, the Friends host the Spring Migration Celebration to welcome the return of the birds. In June, the Design Alaska Wild Arts Walk brings together local artists and the public to showcase nature-inspired artwork. Creamer's Dairy Day in July celebrates the history of the

* See Appendix C: Average Date of First Arrival for Interior Alaska Migratory Birds.

Tanana Valley Sandhill Crane Festival (2022). Friends of Creamer's Field Photo Archives.

dairy years. During the summer months, visitors and locals alike participate in guided nature walks while the end of August brings the annual Tanana Valley Sandhill Crane Festival, a multi-day celebration of the fall crane migration with lectures by nationally-recognized crane experts and artists. Fall and winter events include Creepy Critters in October, Thanksgiving for the Birds in November, and finally, December's Holiday Craft Nights and the Luminary Trail.

In addition to scheduled events, Friends of Creamer's Field members have revived some of the farm's legacy. In 1995, when ADF&G delivered topsoil from land cleared for an addition, volunteers began a community garden on the site of Anna Creamer's once-prolific vegetable plot.

In April 1998, Friends of Creamer's Field purchased the 1935 Case Model L Tractor the Creamers used from 1935 until the close of the farm in 1966. David Nester, who lived on Chena Hot Springs Road, had purchased the tractor at the farm auction in 1967, but by 1998 it

Creamer's Field barn during the annual Luminary Walk (circa 2024). Friends of Creamer's Field Photo Archives.

needed a great deal of work. Through a stroke of good fortune, Robert Moore, the owner of Moore's Antique Tractors and a retired Case dealer from Missouri, visited family in Fairbanks and took on the task of supervising the restoration process, volunteering his time and knowledge during the summer of 1998. He returned in 2000 to help finish the restoration.

Alaska Songbird Institute field station (fall 2024). Alaska Songbird Institute Archives.

In 2001, restoration began on a 1910 Chalmers-Detroit Model K Runabout Charlie Creamer had inherited from his father. The old car had been relegated to Don's garage because of a burned-out clutch. John Wright and Sam Patten of ADF&G oversaw the restoration project, with Carl Gaul from the Vintage Engine Club as the lead mechanic. During the next Golden Days Parade in Fairbanks, Don Creamer rode in it, as his father and mother had done in years past. The tradition now continues with Don's son Jeffery Creamer driving the Chalmers ahead of the Golden Days Parade as part of the Vernon Nash Antique Auto Club. The Chalmers is on display at the Fountainhead Antique Auto Museum.

To direct future progress, the Friends of Creamer's Field Board of Directors developed a strategic plan that states, "The mission of Friends of Creamer's Field is to inspire environmental stewardship and lifelong learning through experience, awareness, and appreciation and conservation of the natural and historical resources of Creamer's Field Migratory Waterfowl Refuge." The goals outlined include a complete renovation of the barns, the development of an auditorium in the creamery, and the construction of additional

Birch leaves litter the Boreal Forest Trail in the fall (2021). Friends of Creamer's Field Photo Archives.

trails. Friends of Creamer's Field cooperates with refuge staff to meet its stated objectives for public education.

ADF&G Manages Farmland for the Birds

Managing the fields and ponds for the benefit of cranes and waterfowl is, of course, a primary objective of ADF&G at Creamer's Field. By clearing snow from the fields and spreading grain, the department provides a safe feeding stopover for thousands of weary birds each spring.

Encouraging waterfowl to nest on the refuge is increasingly a management objective. For although the refuge attracts waterfowl in the spring and fall, it has historically lacked the ponds needed for shoreline nesting sites. Many years before the State purchased the refuge, the Creamers extracted peat northwest of the farmhouse, resulting in a pond that fills with water each spring and supports a lush growth of sedges and other natural vegetation. Once the lake bottom thaws in June, the water percolates into the soil—hence the name, Seasonal Pond. It is attractive to spring waterfowl because it is rich in aquatic life, but in summer, it typically dries up, becoming unsuitable for nesting ducks and geese seeking the safety that open water provides for their young.

In 1984, a neighboring farmer to the north, George Dornath, approached ADF&G and asked for permission to drain water from a wet field onto the refuge. ADF&G consented, and the resulting pond retained water throughout the summer, attracting nesting birds. This success prompted ADF&G to add additional ponds. Using State duck stamp funds to match a $35,000 grant from Ducks Unlimited, ADF&G built six ponds on the northeastern section of the refuge in 1987. Designed with small islands toward the center, these one- to three-acre ponds provide desirable nesting habitat and encourage waterfowl to remain on the refuge throughout the summer. Seed crops planted around the perimeter of the ponds provide forage. The ponds have been successful in attracting nesting birds and are a favorite spot for hunters during the fall.

In March 1988, ADF&G entered into an agreement with the Fairbanks International Airport, the Alaska Department of Transportation and Public Facilities, the University of Alaska Fairbanks School of Agriculture and Land Resource Management, the United States Army Corp of Engineers, and the United States Fish and Wildlife Service to address concerns about cranes and waterfowl at the Fairbanks Airport. Located adjacent to the Tanana and Chena Rivers, Fairbanks International Airport has a float pond, sloughs, and flooded gravel pits that offer appealing habitats for a variety of waterfowl. The University of Alaska agricultural fields, just two miles west of the airport, have traditionally supported migrant waterfowl and cranes. These birds typically flew over the airport twice a day, roosting in the evenings along the Tanana River and flying back over the airport to feed at the university fields during the day. The task force agreed to "eliminate attractive habitat for Lesser Sandhill Cranes at the Airport and to develop replacement habitat" at the refuge.

Under the agreement with the airport and other concerned parties, ADF&G built a pond northeast of the farmhouse in 1989, which came to be called the Sandhill Crane Pond. Used by cranes and waterfowl, the pond offers birds a diet of plants and aquatic insects. It also allows for preening and bathing, with trees along the edge of the viewing fields providing seclusion. As an added measure, the managed fields and Sandhill Crane Pond are under greater restrictions than the rest of the refuge and are closed to public access in the fall to avoid disturbing fall migrants.

The success of these ponds led ADF&G to consider creating additional ponds in the front fields along College Road. Most of the waterfowl using the refuge in the spring and fall are drawn to the front fields because of the grain that is spread there and because the open fields allow the birds to watch for predators. In 1998, ADF&G cleared brush from a natural depression in the east front viewing field and formed the Kessel Pond (named for University of Alaska Fairbanks professor and ornithologist Brina Kessel). Then ADF&G built a series of three additional plastic-

Overlooking the front viewing fields on a spring day. Photograph by Pamela Bergmann.

lined ponds, beginning with a 150,000-gallon pond in the fall of 1999 followed by a 210,000-gallon pond in the fall of 2000 and a 150,000-gallon pond in the fall of 2002.

Refuge Field Management

Because uncultivated fields in Interior Alaska revert to forested lands without continued farming, ADF&G initially leased the refuge fields to area farmers for haying. From 1983 until 1993, the North Pole High School Future Farmers of America harvested hay in the fields. ADF&G assumed all farm management in 1994 (when Future Farmers of America moved on to other projects) and now produces much of the barley that attracts the birds each spring and fall.

In April, when snow still covers the fields, a grader pushes the snow into furrows, exposing the dark soil to speed up snowmelt and produce meltwater ponds. Volunteers from the Borealis Kiwanis Club spread barley on these open furrows. Well water is used to fill the front ponds when snowmelt does not adequately do the job. Snow Buntings kick off the spring migration, arriving at the beginning of April. By the first week of May, the spring migration is typically at its peak. On an average spring day, 2,000–3,000 birds utilize the fields, vocalizing, feeding, and moving in and out of the ponds.

Approximately 200 acres of fields are actively farmed with a rotation of mature barley, sprouting barley, brome grass, fallow, oats, and peas for waterfowl and crane foraging. The health and longevity of the fields are vital to the planting operations. Soil samples are taken from the fields, and fields are occasionally planted with brome grass instead of barley for two to three years. They are then replanted with barley when nutrient levels and organics stabilize or increase. Using a minimum tillage approach to reduce soil loss, fertilizer is spread on the fields, then green crops, such as brome grass, are incorporated as green manure to increase the soil's organic matter and recycle nutrients. Beginning in 2025, ADF&G began no-till drill to seed the fields without disturbing the soil.

Another means of recycling nutrients is through prescribed burns. Each year, the Alaska Department of Natural Resources Division of Forestry conducts controlled burns on the refuge fields to reduce vegetation buildup, enhance grass and sedge growth to recycle nutrients, train wildland firefighters, and demonstrate to the public the ecological role of wildfires.

Alaska Department of Fish and Game managing the fields (2022). Friends of Creamer's Field Photo Archives.

Managing the Refuge for Multi-Use

During the first few years of operations, ADF&G turned down a variety of requests from the local business community for permission to set up businesses on the refuge, including a gravel operation, a golf course, a driving range, and a skeet range. However, the refuge does host groups with different and sometimes conflicting interests.

The Alaska Dog Mushers Association (ADMA) has had one of the longest relationships with Creamer's Field. ADMA has maintained mushing trails and conducted races at Creamer's Field and the surrounding State lands since 1946. Each March, these trails are run by many of the best teams in the world during the Open North American Championship Sled Dog Races. These trails also benefit many skiers, skijorers, and snow machiners.

Hunting and trapping are allowed in designated areas with prior registration at ADF&G. Moose hunting is allowed by bow or muzzleloader through a registration or drawing permit, and ADF&G recommends traps and snares not be set within 30 feet of ski or mushing trails. However, trapping beaver is prohibited on the refuge as ADF&G wishes to encourage beaver activity there.

The use of off-road vehicles is prohibited except during the winter months, when snow machines are allowed on refuge trails. Because of its central location, the refuge provides links to Goldstream Valley, Chena Hot Springs Road, and the Chena River. Without access to refuge trails, riders would be required to travel many miles out of their way to reach these trails. However, snow machine use on the refuge has long been a source of contention among user groups and refuge staff.

Facility and Site Improvements

Record-setting snowfall in the winter of 1991–1992 damaged the refuge's barns, and staff realized they needed to either address the historically significant buildings or lose them altogether. The tremendous weight of the winter snow forced the walls of the older, taller barn to bow outward, and bullet holes shot through the roof several years before had left the interior of the barn vulnerable to water damage. Emergency repairs were made to stabilize the barns, and in 2001, both barns and the creamery were re-roofed. Much work remains to be done if the barn and creamery are ever to be used for exhibits and classrooms, but, for now, the buildings are in stable condition.

The access to Creamer's Field Migratory Refuge, along College Road, received a major facelift in 1996 through funding from a federal highways program, the Intermodal Surface Transportation Efficiency Act (ISTEA). With this grant, the entrance to the refuge was redesigned,

A musher rounds a bend at Creamer's Field in the 2023 Open North American Sled Dog Race. Friends of Creamer's Field Photo Archives.

allowing cars to enter at the Danby Road traffic light, west of the original entrance. Overhead utility lines leading from College Road to the dairy buildings were relocated underground to restore the dairy's original appearance. The project added more visitor parking and three viewing platforms, replaced old and rotting wooden viewing stands with ones that are handicapped accessible, improved the nature path, built a ramp to the farmhouse entrance, and installed a replica of the historic fence in front of the farmhouse.

The ADF&G district office building also underwent changes during the 1990s. Staff numbers had increased since 1971, when the district office relocated to the refuge, and new office and storage space was needed. The Alaska legislature appropriated funding in 1995, and an addition went up to the north side of the building, nearly doubling the square footage. The addition was completed in 1997.

Additions to the Refuge

Over the years, ADF&G acquired additional land for the refuge. Beginning with the 259-acre homestead, 12 acres including the farmhouse and barns, and 1,493 acres transferred from adjacent state lands, they subsequently purchased 56 acres from the Sherman Trust in 1999, 40 acres from farmer George Dornath in August 2001, and an additional 120 acres from Ken Mendes in 2010. ADF&G then partnered with The Conservation Fund to purchase an additional 688 acres between 2020 and 2023. All additional lands are contiguous and encompass a mosaic of ponds, forests, and cultivated fields, providing habitat for Sandhill Cranes, waterfowl, owls, hawks, grouse, woodpeckers, migrant and resident songbirds, and mammals such as

Shoring the oldest barn after heavy snowfall (circa 2001). Photograph by Len Kamerling, Friends of Creamer's Field Photo Archives.

foxes, snowshoe hares, and moose. The State of Alaska Department of Natural Resources owns all refuge lands, but ADF&G manages them under a cooperative agreement. With these additions, almost 2,700 acres are now managed according to the goals, policies, and regulations of Creamer's Field Migratory Waterfowl Refuge. Further acreage along the south-west border of the refuge is owned by the Alaska Department of Natural Resources but managed by ADF&G.

Future Management Plans

In the early 1990s, ADF&G completed a major planning effort for the refuge, resulting in the 1992 Interpretive Plan, the 1993 Interim Management Plan, and the 1994 Facilities Plan. These plans continue as the template for management practices at the refuge. The management goals for the refuge are:

1. To protect and enhance the quality and diversity of habitat for wildlife with special emphasis on waterfowl and other migratory birds.
2. To protect and enhance the opportunity to view, photograph, and gain an understanding of the ecosystems, including wildlife species, plant species, geological, and other features typical of Interior Alaska.
3. To encourage opportunities for public education about terrestrial and aquatic ecosystems, wildlife, habitat, historical resources, and related topics.
4. To allow other public uses that are consistent with the above statutory purposes and management goals.

Many people offer visions for the future of the refuge. Friends of Creamer's Field dreams of the day when the lovely old barns are restored and will once again host a community barn dance. And Friends hopes to see the creamery upgraded to allow for a large classroom and laboratory. As these improvements are funded and implemented, the refuge will continue to undergo modifications according to the vision of people who value the refuge as a place for the birds and for recreational opportunities within the heart of this northern city.

Woodchucks

In May, the first flush of green coincides with the raucous arrival of waterfowl and songbirds while wood frogs thaw after a miraculous hibernation uttering their "rack-rack" mating call. Mid-summer, moose calves high-step on spindly legs, fuzzy ducklings learn to swim, and Camp Habitat brings yelps of discovery from kids with nets. August heralds fall, as birch and aspens flash gold, and Sandhills circle in preparation for their journey south.

A summer day beckons beyond the bridge over Jussilla Creek. Friends of Creamer's Field Photo Archives.

Winter transforms Creamer's Field. Short days give rise to evening's alpine glow, while snow brightens the landscape, and a network of trails beckons cross-country skiers, solo skijorers, and dog mushers. Although the variety of birds declines significantly, swirling flocks of cheery Redpolls, noisy Boreal and Black-capped Chickadees, melodic White-winged Crossbills, and showy Bohemian Waxwings make every visit a birding adventure.

Luminaries light the way along the bridge over Jussilla Creek. Friends of Creamer's Field Photo Archives.

Violet-Green Swallow

Conclusion

Over a century ago, a small dairy built of logs from the surrounding forest operated near the tiny community of Fairbanks, Alaska. Through the ingenuity, hardships, and quiet pleasures of the Hinckley and Creamer families, the Creamer's Dairy prospered for many years. In its decline, a new purpose for the land took shape. By good fortune and grassroots determination, a small vestige of pioneer Alaska remains.

With its carefully cultivated fields and boardwalk trails (slated for climate-resistant redesign in 2025), Creamer's Field Migratory Waterfowl Refuge is not a wilderness. Yet it offers residents and visitors access to the natural world just minutes from most of the city's homes and offices. The 2,700-acre refuge gives Fairbanks a rural feeling that belies the city's actual size. Without question, Creamer's Field has helped shape a town that is purely Alaskan—where dog mushing occurs in town in the winter and birds congregate each spring after traversing the continent. The city is evolving with a refuge at its core, incorporating wildlife, recreation, and environmental education into mainstream urban life.

The refuge draws people for a variety of reasons. For some, it provides a sense of belonging, as Creamer's Field offers many community-based activities. Others value the solitary adventures they have while mushing, skijoring, hunting, or bird-watching, to name a few of the most common activities visitors enjoy. For some, the history represented by the farm buildings provides a tangible connection to Fairbanks' pioneering past. Certainly, this history provides a reminder of how easily the land could have been put to other uses. These values lend themselves to the sense of place people feel for the refuge.

Fairbanks is a city surrounded by wilderness in all directions. But open spaces worldwide are fast disappearing, and even in Alaska, development will eat away at our open lands. As Fairbanks expands, this historic oasis will continue to offer the community a ready means of protecting and enjoying the wild things we treasure.

Appendices

Appendix A
Average Temperatures, Precipitation and Snowfall

	Jan	Feb	Mar	Apr	May	Jun
Max F	1	10	25	44	61	72
Min F	-17	-13	-3	21	38	49
Inches Precip.	0.58	0.42	0.25	0.31	0.60	1.37
Inches Snow	10	8	5	3	1	0
	Jul	Aug	Sep	Oct	Nov	Dec
Max F	73	66	55	32	11	5
Min F	52	46	35	17	-6	-13
Inches Precip.	2.16	1.88	1.10	0.83	0.67	0.64
Inches Snow	0	0	2	11	13	12

Source: https://www.usclimatedata.com/climate/fairbanks/alaska/united-states/usak0083

Appendix B

Average Date of First Arrival of Migratory Birds

March:	18th	Snow Bunting
	25th	Golden Eagle
April:	12th	Rough-legged Hawk
	13th	Common Goldeneye
	14th	Lapland Longspur
		Short-eared Owl
	15th	Canada Goose
		Northern Pintail
		Red-tailed Hawk
		Northern Harrier
	17th	Mallard
		American Kestrel
	19th	Trumpeter Swan
		Tundra Swan
		Herring Gull
	20th	Greater White-fronted Goose
		American Robin
	22nd	American Wigeon
		Sandhill Crane
		Snow Goose
	23rd	Northern Shoveler
		Ruby-crowned Kinglet
		American Tree Sparrow
		Peregrine Falcon
	24th	Green-winged Teal
		Mew Gull

This list does not include all species, but only those common to the Fairbanks area. Document made available by the Alaska Songbird Institute (http://aksongbird.org). Adapted from Gibson and Kessel, UAMuseum (1991); Alaska Bird Observatory (2009); and ADF&G (2012).

April:	25th	Redhead
		Canvasback
		American Pipit
		Yellow-rumped Warbler
	26th	Barrow's Goldeneye
		Dark-eyed Junco
	27th	Varied Thrush
	28th	Rusty Blackbird
		Fox Sparrow
		Bufflehead
	29th	Sharp-shinned Hawk
		Violet-green Swallow
		Tree Swallow
	30th	Lesser Yellowlegs
May:	1st	Wilson's Snipe
		Bonaparte's Gull
		Northern Flicker
		Hammonds Flycatcher
		Savannah Sparrow
		White-crowned Sparrow
		Hermit Thrush
	2nd	Solitary Sandpiper
	3rd	Golden-crowned Sparrow
		Lincoln's Sparrow
	4th	Horned Grebe
		American Golden Plover
	6th	Red-necked Grebe
		Semipalmated Plover
		Merlin
	7th	Orange-crowned Warbler
		Ring-neck Duck
		Pectoral Sandpiper

May:	7th	Least Sandpiper
		Belted Kingfisher
		Semipalmated Sandpiper
	9th	Lesser Scaup
		Gadwall
	10th	Long-billed Dowitcher
		Townsend's Warbler
		Wilson's Warbler
		Killdeer
	11th	Greater Yellowlegs
		Whimbrel
		Say's Phoebe
		Cliff Swallow
		Horned Lark
	12th	Swainson's Thrush
		Northern Waterthrush
	13th	Upland Sandpiper
		Red-necked Phalarope
		Yellow Warbler
		Blackpoll Warbler
	15th	Grey-cheeked Thrush
	16th	Western Wood Pewee
		Olive-sided Flycatcher
	17th	Hudsonian Godwit
	19th	Bank Swallow
	20th	Blue-winged Teal
		Red-winged Blackbird
	23rd	Wilson's Phalarope
	25th	Alder Flycatcher

Appendix C

Mammals of Creamer's Field

Bat, Little Brown

Bear, Black

Bear, Brown

Beaver

Ermine

Fox, Red

Hare, Snowshoe

Lemming, Northern Bog

Lynx

Marten

Mink

Moose

Mouse, Meadow Jumping

Muskrat

Porcupine

Shrew, Arctic

Shrew, Masked (Common)

Shrew, Pygmy

Squirrel, Northern Flying

Squirrel, Red

Vole, Meadow

Vole, Northern Red-Backed

Vole, Tundra

Weasel, Least

Wolf

Appendix D
Creamer Family Tree

Creamer, Charles Newton (C.N.) -1945

Married date unknown: Mary Jane Todd (Minnie) -1945

- Creamer, Tessie
- Creamer, Camellia
- Creamer, Marian
- Creamer, Frances
- Creamer, Genevieve
- Creamer, Mattie
- **Creamer, Charlie 1889-1974**

  Married 1920: Anastasia Elizabeth Carr (Anna) 1885-1965

  - **Creamer, Donald George (Don) 1922-2003**

    Married 1943: Connie Allyn

    - Creamer, Charles
    - Creamer, Clifford
    - Creamer, Donald
    - Creamer, Jeannie
    - Creamer, Jeffery
    - Creamer, Roxanne

Selected Bibliography Primary Sources

Interviews

Bell, Don, and Don Creamer. Interview by Mark Ross and India Spartz, November 3, 2001, Creamer's Farmhouse, tape recording, University of Alaska, Rasmuson Library Archives, Fairbanks, Alaska.

Anderson, Merwin "Buster." Interview by Robin Lewis, July 18, 1988, tape recording, Creamer's Farmhouse Archives, Fairbanks, Alaska.

Caikoski, Jason R. Interview with author, September 23, 2003, Alaska Department of Fish and Game regional office, Fairbanks, Alaska.

Cole, Terrence. Lecture, January 2003, University of Alaska Museum, Fairbanks, Alaska.

Creamer, Charlie. Interview by Ruth Knapman, fall 1970, tape recording, Knapman personal library, Fairbanks, Alaska.

Creamer, Charlie. Interview by Mike Dalton, June 1973, Fairbanks Pioneer Home, tape recording, Creamer's Farmhouse Archives, Fairbanks, Alaska.

Creamer, Charlie. Interview by Robin Lewis. June 29, 1988, tape recording, Creamer's Farmhouse Archives, Fairbanks, Alaska.

Creamer, Don, Jeannie Creamer, Roxie Creamer. Public lecture, April 2, 1992, Noel Wien Library, tape recording, Creamer's Farmhouse Archives, Fairbanks, Alaska.

Creamer, Don. Interview by Mark Ross and India Spartz, November 10, 2001, Creamer's Farmhouse, tape recording, University of Alaska Rasmuson Library Archives, Fairbanks, Alaska.

Creamer-Dalton, Jeannie. Interview with author, April 19, 2003, Gulliver's Books, Fairbanks, Alaska.

Guthrie, Dale. Public lecture, March 31, 2003, Noel Wien Library, tape recording, University of Alaska, Museum Archives, Fairbanks, Alaska.

Hunter, Celia. Public meeting, May 4, 1985, tape recording, University of Alaska Rasmuson Library Archives, Fairbanks, Alaska.

Inglis, Betty. Public lecture, March 31, 2003, Noel Wien Library, tape recording, University of Alaska Museum Archives, Fairbanks, Alaska.

Knapman, Ruth. Public lecture, April 7, 2003, Noel Wien Library, Fairbanks Alaska.

Krauss, Michael. Phone interview by author, March 27, 2003, Fairbanks, Alaska.

Mayo, Gail. Interview with author, May 5, 2003, Gulliver's Books, Fairbanks, Alaska.

Stroecker, Bill. Lecture, 2002, Anne Wien Elementary School, Fairbanks, Alaska.

Stoltz, Susan Grace. Interview with author, May 9, 2003, Creamer's Field Farmhouse, Fairbanks, Alaska.

Wright, John. Interview with author, May 14, 2003, Alaska Department of Fish and Game Regional Office, Fairbanks, Alaska.

Wright, John. Interview with author, June 5, 2003, Alaska Department of Fish and Game regional office, Fairbanks, Alaska.

Books

Murie, Margaret E. *Two in the Far North*, Anchorage, Seattle and Portland: Alaska Northwest Books, 1978.

Newspaper References

The Fairbanks Miner, Vol. 1, No. 1, May 1903.

Fairbanks Daily News-Miner, 1919–1989.

Periodicals

Alaska Conservation Society News Bulletin, May 1967.

Alaska Conservation Society News Bulletin, Spring 1968.

Unpublished Materials

Friends of Creamer's Field Strategic Plan 2002–2007.

Archival Sources

Creamer, Anna. Unpublished diary entry, undated. Creamer's Farmhouse Archives, Fairbanks, Alaska.

Carr, Anna and Louis Golden. Marriage Certificate for, October 2, 1904, District of Alaska, Third Judicial Division, Fairbanks, Alaska. Creamer's Farmhouse Archives, Fairbanks, Alaska.

Murray, E.G. and Charles Hinckley. Notarized deed transferring title of the land from Murray to Hinckley dated January 3, 1910. Creamer's Farmhouse Archives, Fairbanks, Alaska.

Golden, Anna and Charles Creamer. Marriage Certificate for October 16, 1920, Seattle Washington. Creamer's Farmhouse Archives, Fairbanks, Alaska.

Hinckley, Charles. Court records, City of Fairbanks, Alaska, granting ownership of homestead.

Hinckley, Charles. Letter dated March 25, 1915, accompanying application for a homestead. Creamer's Farmhouse Archives, Fairbanks, Alaska.

Government Documents

_______, "Creamer's Field Migratory Waterfowl Refuge, Interim Management Plan." Fairbanks: Alaska Department of Fish and Game, March 1993, photocopied.

_______, Property record Serial #0377, Patent #566467, May 11, 1973. Fairbanks North Star Borough Recorder's Office.

Caikoski, Jason R. "Fairbanks International Airport Bird Management Project, 2002 Progress Report." Fairbanks: Alaska Department of Fish and Game, December 2002, photocopied.

Caikoski, Jason R. "Farming Operations 2002, Creamer's Field Migratory Waterfowl Refuge, Alaska." Fairbanks: Department of Fish and Game, Division of Wildlife Conservation, December 2002, photocopied.

Murphy, Nancy. "Fairbanks Wildlife Management Area: the Human Use Aspect." Fairbanks: Alaska Department of Fish and Game, fall 1975, photocopied.

Selected Bibliography Secondary Sources

Books

Berton, Pierre. *Klondike Fever.* New York: Carroll and Graf Publishers, 1974.

Brooks, Alfred Hulse. *Blazing Alaska's Trails.* Fairbanks: University of Alaska and the Arctic Institute of North America, 1953 reprint, Fairbanks: University of Alaska Press, 1973.

Cole, Dermot. *City History Series; Fairbanks, A Gold Rush Town That Beat The Odds.* Fairbanks, Seattle: Epicenter Press, 1999.

Cole, Terrence. *Crooked Past–The History of a Frontier Mining Camp, Fairbanks, Alaska.* Fairbanks: University of Alaska Press, 1991.

DuPuis, E. Melanie. *Nature's Perfect Food, How Milk Became America's Drink.* New York and London: New York University Press, 2002.

Johnsgard, Paul A. *Crane Music–A Natural History of American Cranes.* Washington and London: Smithsonian Institution Press, 1984.

Naske, Claus-M. and Herman E. Slotnick. *Alaska, A History of the 49th State, 2d ed.* Norman and London: University of Oklahoma Press, 1987.

Ross, Ken. *Environmental Conflict in Alaska.* Boulder: University Press of Colorado, 2000.

Tuan, Yi-Fu. *Space and Place, The Perspective of Experience.* Minneapolis: University of Minnesota, 1977.

Wold, Jo Anne. *Fairbanks, the $200 million Gold Rush Town.* Fairbanks: Wold Press, 1971.

Wold, Jo Anne. *The Way it Was, Of People, Places and Things In Pioneer Interior Alaska.* Anchorage: Alaska Northwest Publishing Company, 1988.

Newspaper References

Fairbanks Daily News-Miner, 1959.

Periodicals

Lewis, Robin. "The History of Creamer's Dairy-Fairbanks Alaska," Alaska Magazine (2nd ed. 1990).

Miller, E. Willard. "Agricultural Development in Interior Alaska," Scientific Monthly (October 1951): 245-254.

Cole, Terrence, ed. "Nome City of the Golden Beaches," Alaska Geographic Society (Vol. II, Number 1, 1984).

Spencer, J.E. and R.J. Horvath. "How Does an Agricultural Region Originate?" Annals, Association of American Geographers (1963).

Williams, Daniel R. and Susan I. Stewart. "Sense of Place, An Elusive Concept That is Finding a Home in Ecosystem Management," Journal of Forestry (May 1998): 18 - 23.

Unpublished Materials

Price, Kathy. "Homesteads on Fort Wainwright." Ft. Collins: Colorado State University, Center for Environmental Management of Military Lands, September 2002.

Robe, Cecil Francis. "The Penetration of an Alaskan Frontier: The Tanana Valley and Fairbanks." Ph.D. diss., Yale University, 1943.

Shortridge, James R. "American Perceptions of the Agricultural Potential of Alaska, 1867–1958." Ph.D. diss., University of Kansas, 1972.

Spindler, Michael Andrew. "Ecological Survey of the Birds, Mammals and Vegetation of Fairbanks Wildlife Management Area." Master's Thesis, University of Alaska, Fairbanks, 1976.

Williams, Daniel R. and Michael E. Patterson. "Environmental Psychology: Mapping Landscape Meanings for Ecosystem Management." Fort Collins: Fifth International Symposium on Society and Natural Resource Management, June 7–10, 1994.

Archival Sources

Knapman, Ruth. "The Story of Creamer's Dairy." Fairbanks: Tanana–Yukon Historical Society, 1984, photocopied.

Online Sources

Alaska Department of Fish and Game

https://www.adfg.alaska.gov/index.cfm?adfg=creamersfield.main
https://www.adfg.alaska.gov/static/lands/protectedareas/_land_status_maps/creamersfieldls.pdf
https://www.adfg.alaska.gov/static/home/library/pdfs/wildlife/research_pdfs/creamers_field_migratory_waterfowl_refuge_winter_guide.pdf

Friends of Creamer's Field

https://friendsofcreamersfield.org
https://www.facebook.com/friendsofcreamersfield
https://www.instagram.com/Friendsofcreamersfield
https://www.youtube.com/@friendsofcreamersfield

Wikipedia

https://en.wikipedia.org/wiki/Creamer%27s_Field_Migratory_Waterfowl_Refuge

All Trails

https://www.alltrails.com/parks/us/alaska/creamers-field-state-game-refuge

The Conservation Fund

https://www.conservationfund.org/our-impact/projects/creamers-field-how-an-alaskan-dairy-farm-became-a-wildlife-sanctuary

Alaska.org

https://www.alaska.org/detail/creamers-field

Cornell Lab of Ornithology

https://ebird.org/hotspot/L128537

https://www.allaboutbirds.org/news/event/spring-migration-celebration/

Alaska Songbird Institute

https://aksongbird.org/wp-content/uploads/2018/08/ACTIVITYBOOK-2018.pdf

StoryMaps

https://storymaps.arcgis.com/stories/49bc1224cd064da6a5c0fbe0029bfcde

iNaturalist

https://www.inaturalist.org/observations?nelat=64.8646754802915&nelng=-147.7368315697085&swlat=64.861977519708496&swlng=-147.7395295302915

Index

Index

About the Author

As a naturalist in Alaska's boreal and marine ecosystems, Jessica A. Shepherd has published essays in *49 Writers, Alaska Women Speak, Humans of the World, Sad Girls Club,* and *Hip Pocket Press*. She holds a BA in Environmental Biology from the University of Colorado Boulder, an MA in Northern Studies from the University of Alaska Fairbanks, and an MFA in Creative Writing, non-fiction, from the University of Alaska Anchorage. She resides in Homer, Alaska, with her husband and two oversized lap dogs.

www.ingramcontent.com/pod-product-compliance
Ingram Content Group UK Ltd.
Pitfield, Milton Keynes, MK11 3LW, UK
UKHW021837270726
14058UKWH00002B/194